COMMON
Threads

*Why The Answers to the
Present Lie in the Past*

MELISSA COLLINS HARRELL

One Printers Way
Altona, MB R0G 0B0
Canada

www.friesenpress.com

Copyright © 2022 by Melissa Collins Harrell
First Edition — 2022

All rights reserved.

Scripture quotations are from the New Revised Standard Version Bible, copyright © 1989 the Division of Christian Education of the National Council of the Churches of Christ in the United States of America. Used by permission. All rights reserved.

No part of this publication may be reproduced in any form, or by any means, electronic or mechanical, including photocopying, recording, or any information browsing, storage, or retrieval system, without permission in writing from FriesenPress.

ISBN
978-1-03-914204-6 (Hardcover)
978-1-03-914203-9 (Paperback)
978-1-03-914205-3 (eBook)

1. BIOGRAPHY & AUTOBIOGRAPHY, PERSONAL MEMOIRS

Distributed to the trade by The Ingram Book Company

COMMON
Threads

Table of Contents

Prologue	1
Introduction	3
Letter and Invitation to My Reader	5
A Guide to the Book	7
Build Your Coping Kit	10
Biology 101 Basics	12
Vulnerability	15
The Invisible Line	17
Tapping In	21
Responsibility	27
Begin at the Beginning	29
Running from Insanity	35
Groceries and Throw Downs	39
Moxie Meets Kevin	41
A Call for Healing	43
Caregiving Gene	46
The Invisible Workforce	49
The Mother Load	52
Unexpected Gifts	56
Competency	63
Moonshine, Mayberry, and Mechanics	65
Replicating Emergency! for Mental Health	68
Digging Deep	73
Dancing Dreams	75
You're Going to Major in What?	81
Finding My Way	85
The Power of Words	88
The Crowning Moment	93
Gleaning the Good	96
The Making of a Therapist	99

Finding My Mind	104
Jesus Saved Me, Dancing Healed Me	109
You Can't Get There from Here	112
Sweet Stella, Sunscreen, and Swahili	118
Never Judge a Book, or a Child by Its Cover	122
Achievement	**127**
My Isaac Moment	129
Turning Points	132
Disaster Recovery Round One	136
I Only Iron For Jesus	138
Return to the Wilderness	143
Disaster Recovery Round Two	147
Survival	**153**
Shock and Denial	155
Frogs and Princes	161
Anger/Bargaining	166
Control	**169**
The Art of Being Conned	171
Magnolia Tribe	174
The Aftermath	180
Fight, Flight, Freeze	183
Where Does My Help Come From?	187
Waking Up to Abuse	190
Refined by Fire	195
Holiday Hell	200
From Practice to Pandemic	203
One Brave Koi Fish	206
The Last Goodbye	214
Irreconcilable Differences	217
Worse than Death	221
Justice	224
Acceptance	229
Epilogue	**235**

"There is some task which the God of all the Universe, the Great Creator, your Redeemer in Jesus Christ has for you to do--and which will remain undone and incomplete until, by faith and obedience, you step into the will of God."

—Alan Redpath

DEDICATION

I have been blessed to encounter wonderful people in my life who get up every day and persevere through unimaginable struggles. Whether family or complete strangers, your stories are forever written on my heart. Your ability to endure suffering has inspired me and given me strength to press on, even when I'm weary from my own trials. May this work bring about awareness and invite systemic change so that your struggles were never in vain. Finally, to the three humans I get the privilege to call my own: Landry, Spencer Grace, and Jonah—you will always be living proof of an awesome God, the biology of resilience, and my greatest gifts.

Prologue

August 8, 2019

I reach for a towel to dry my hands and glance at the clock. Yes, success! I will not be late today! I place the top on the fruit tray I just arranged for my staff meeting. Certainly not Pinterest worthy but hopefully something to brighten the day.

Food secure, I now begin the frantic search for shoes and keys, all while making a mental note to myself to return said items to their designated homes each day. A pointless effort I've attempted since college but clearly to no avail. Mental note erased. I finally find my shoes while, somewhere under weeks of work, I hear the vibration of a phone. After an archeological dig through a pile of work reports, I find the device that demands to be answered.

Correct buzzing device in hand, I glance to decide if I have the time to spare for the caller at the other end. It's my husband. Ok, for him I have a minute to spare for a quick conversation. Our lives have always been busy with career building, family struggles, and eventually three kids, but after twenty-six years together, I still always want to talk to him. He's not only my husband but also my best friend.

Melissa Collins Harrell

As soon as I hit accept and say hello, I notice a tone in his voice that I've only heard at one other time in my life—the day he told me my dad had died. My heart races. At this moment I know that whatever he's about to tell me, our lives will never be the same.

Introduction

Letter and Invitation to My Reader

IN AUGUST OF 2019, I experienced a traumatic experience so deep that it made me question every piece of my life. I was left stripped completely bare of all I thought I knew about myself and the world around me. My life was crushed, and all my future hopes and dreams seemed to disappear in an instant. All that was left for me to do was to get up each day and simply exist—a robotic existence void of joy and peace. In my mind, life was over, and I would never be whole again.

As I attempted to process all the heavy pain and confusion, I turned to a coping skill I have used since childhood. From the moment I first held a pencil, I've been a writer. The act of writing has always been a tool to process my feelings, release pain, and map out my next steps. My love for words has led to overflowing bookshelves, a closet full of journals, and a sick addiction to office supplies. I fear that one day I will be "that lady" on the nightly news who ran back into her flaming house, not to save her cat, but to save her journals and possibly a large box of gel pens.

I'm not only a writer but also a trauma therapist. So how does a trauma therapist sort through her own trauma? I wish all that expensive education and training could have made my pain and struggle less, but the human heart is the same no matter your profession. In trauma therapy we use a term: trauma threads. If we follow the line, they'll lead us to the root belief that holds all this trauma together in the proverbial ball of yarn. Our families of origin and difficult events leave scars. These scars lead us to create negative coping patterns that become unconscious default mechanisms. The way we interact and respond in our current situations is likely rooted in very old memories and experiences.

Like a wilderness explorer, I set off on a personal quest in search of my trauma roots. To resolve my current distress, I needed to understand my life and how I became who I was at this moment. This book is the product of a complex voyage fraught with traveling to my childhood stomping grounds, digging through mountains of family photos, interviewing relatives, and plodding through years of journals, all while simultaneously writing new life chapters. Like the butterfly in the cocoon I grew, struggled, and fought my way out of darkness through solo traveling, attending therapy, and wrestling with my faith like no time ever before. Throughout my whole life, my faith had been a huge tethering root, but this crisis with a hurricane force wind had completely unearthed those roots, leaving me feeling the most exposed and empty.

A Guide to the Book

WHILE I'VE ALWAYS HARBORED the secret desire to write more books, this is most definitely not the next one I thought I'd write. This book, perhaps by providence, simply emerged along my healing path. It's by no means a fix-your-life-in-thirty-days book, nor was this work ever intended to be an academic textbook. As therapists, we learn and work from an eclectic stance, which means that we pull from various theories and skills. None of the concepts in this book do I claim as my own theories or ideas; this is simply a window into the work. Where indicated, proper acknowledgement is given to authors or theorists, and a simple list of references for deeper investigation is included in the back. While this list is by no means exhaustive related to trauma and resiliency, it will give you a good starting point.

At various points in my life, people have told me that I'm one of the strongest people they've ever met. I often get the sense that people believe that grit or personal strength is like a gene, and that some people are just naturally strong. The truth is, every single person has what they need within them to get through what life throws at them. We don't realize it at the time, but every single life experience creates opportunities to build our resilience muscles. Later when adversity arises yet again, we tap into those lessons learned to help us survive.

Each reader will be in different life situations. While I'm a licensed therapist, this book is also not intended to replace professional support by a mental health professional. As you'll see between these covers, even therapists need the support of a professional at times. This work is simply me sharing my human struggles as well as my professional experiences of working with others through suffering. It's one thing to share my stories and struggles in a journal, with friends in crisis, or even speaking to small audiences, but this is a whole other level of vulnerability. However, I believe this willingness to become vulnerable to one another is what will eventually bring the most healing to us individually and as a society.

Trauma is so prevalent in our world and the root cause of so many personal and societal struggles. Much healing needs to take place, and we already possess the seeds inside of us … we just need a little water and sunlight of instruction to get us growing. It's my deepest desire that sharing my experiences and tangled threads will help others to feel validated in their pain and allow themselves permission to do the work necessary to heal. It's long past time to make mental health care equitable to other health issues and create a society that encourages people to prioritize theirs.

The book is divided into the following sections: vulnerability, responsibility, competency, achievement, survival, and control. These are the areas of cognitions where we most often hold our negative distortions about ourselves. Unconsciously, these negative beliefs influence us every day. In Cognitive Behavioral Therapy, created by Dr. Aaron Beck, we teach our clients to identify the negative cognition such as "I'm a failure," and then we invite our clients to challenge these beliefs. Once challenged, we reframe it as a positive belief, such as "I'm trying the best I can."

Most clients are relieved to learn that we all have developed some form of faulty thinking patterns.

In Eye Movement Desensitization and Reprocessing (EMDR) therapy, created by Dr. Francine Shapiro, we take it a step further. EMDR recognizes that not only have our brains been impacted by negative experiences, but our body holds these events and memories. We've all had the experience of riding in our car and a song comes on that takes you to a special time in your life, or a scent makes you think of a happy memory. Just as these pleasant memories are activated by the five senses, negative events and memories get triggered in the same way. Through unlocking the physical manifestations and tapping into the positive cognitions, the brain learns not to access these negative experiences so readily.

Build Your Coping Kit

MY CAREER PATH, ALONG with some early adversities, has given me access to skills that support personal resilience. The title *Common Threads* refers to trauma threads, but it also has a deep personal meaning for me. This title is a tribute to my Western NC history full of women who quilted and sewed beautiful works of art while enduring with incredible strength and grace their fair share of adversity. All these women had sewing boxes full of threads, scissors, and all kinds of nifty tools that helped them as they created their beautiful creations.

This book is filled with a variety of tools that have sustained me along the way, and I hope they assist you in building your resilience toolbox of sorts. Possessing resilience skills is not a magic wand to poof you through the hard times. Rather, these skills sustain you as you move minute by minute, hour by hour through to the other side. Each tool will be highlighted with a sewing symbol beside it for easy reference.

The first tool I invite you to start using is what created this work: journaling. If you've never journaled before, it can seem like a scary task. Simply begin with paper or your computer and write whatever comes to your mind. It may only be a few sentences. Don't judge what you write—just write. As you begin, don't treat it like homework; just write as you feel led to write. As time moves on, you'll notice that you crave and miss it when you don't journal.

Set a time of day that works for you. Before I had children, I loved journaling at the end of the day to sort through my thoughts and plans for the next day. Once I had children, I changed to journaling in the morning with my coffee, or else it would never happen. You may find that the only time you can grab it is at your desk during a lunch break. Obviously feeling free to write openly is important, so it may be that you want to type on a device that allows your work to be password protected.

One of the gifts of journaling is the ability to go back and see growth in yourself and recognize your blessings. Each year on my birthday, I read through the previous year's journal and acknowledge all the prayers that were answered for myself and those I prayed over. In this fast-paced society, it's easy to move from one problem to the next without acknowledging what we've accomplished and what worked out for us by the mystery of faith. In these hindsight reflections we can often see how God showed up in ways that we were not prepared to acknowledge in the moment. It's a humbling experience in gratitude. Along the way you'll find prompts to encourage your journaling process.

Biology 101 Basics

IT TRULY ALL BEGINS with the breath. The breath is so fundamental to life that we will die without oxygen within minutes of cessation of breathing. I didn't truly learn the power of breath work until my first disaster recovery job in 2017. Up until this point, I really didn't have a lot of faith in taking deep breaths. I know ... an embarrassing thing for this veteran therapist to now admit. I sure wasn't buying it related to childbirth and would have preordered my epidural via DoorDash had that existed back in my baby-delivery days. In the past, if someone told me, "Just calm down; take a deep breath," it was like a trigger for me. It honestly made me want to slap them. I felt like my situation was being minimized and I was being treated like a child who was overreacting.

As I began to work with survivors of Hurricane Matthew, I was so overwhelmed. This catastrophic storm brought so much damage to our communities by way of historic flooding. In all my years of clinical work, I had never worked with people who needed so much so fast. They had not only lost their homes but also hope. One day in a regional meeting, I told my supervisor that I was just at a loss of how best to support survivors. My supervisor looked at me and said, "Are you consistently teaching breathing techniques?" I'm not sure exactly what my facial expression transmitted to her, but in my mind I thought, *These people just had their entire life washed down the river, and you want me to tell them to take a deep breath!* If they felt the same way as me, I would most definitely need to prepare to get slapped multiple times. I guess a look was worth a thousand words because her response was, "I know, Melissa, it doesn't seem like much, but it will take their bodies off fight or flight, which is the number one priority right now."

The rate of our breath guides our body in many ways. When we're in a calm state, our breath is normal, our muscles relaxed, and our heart rate regular. We refer to this state as our "rest and digest" mode. When we experience a stressful event, our body goes into fight, flight, or freeze mode. The heart rate increases, breathing becomes shallower, and many other body systems shut down to allow the body to protect itself. The brain has one mission and one mission only—to survive.

Deep in our brain we have a fire alarm of sorts called the amygdala. When the body goes into fight or flight mode, the amygdala sends out the alarm to prepare our body for battle. When we draw a deep breath in and exhale slowly out, we send signals to the brain that turn the alarm off and let the body know that all is well. When you learn that you can regulate your breath and calm your body off of fight or flight, you gain a sense of power and control like nothing else. Anxiety thrives on fear and lack of control, so when you take those back, you're the winner every time. We always have our breath with us, and it's free to use.

Resilience Skill: Breath Work Practice

Find a comfortable place to sit.

Close your eyes or glance down at the floor.

Melissa Collins Harrell

Begin to focus on your breath and notice the rate of your breath.

Don't try to change it; just become aware of it.

Pretend you're holding a cupcake with a lit candle in it.

Begin to bring your breath in through your nose and then exhale out through your mouth, as if you're blowing out a birthday candle. Blow the breath out slow and sustained, as if you're trying to make the birthday candle flicker but not go out.

Begin to deepen your breath, bringing more air deep into your lungs and belly. Then exhale slowly out for longer periods of time.

Incorporate this practice throughout your day. It can be done when you wake up or while you're dressing, waiting in lines, or driving in your car (eyes open please!). The more you incorporate, the more you'll get the benefits.

Your situation, just like you, is unique. Only you can know what you need, but second by second, breath by breath, you will make it. I promise you this: as hard as it is to believe, one day you'll do more than exist. But for today, dear friend, that's enough. Breathe in … breathe out … and congratulate yourself for the bravery just to take each breath.

Vulnerability

The Invisible Line

"All the world's a stage,
And all the men and women merely players.
They have their exits and their entrances.
And one man in his time plays many parts ..."

—William Shakespeare (*As You Like It*, Act 2, Scene 7)

IN THE THEATER WE have a saying: "Bad dress rehearsal, good show." Dress rehearsals give us the opportunity to correct unforeseen issues before we get to the live performance. In life, there are no dress rehearsals; you have to take whatever comes your way and somehow muddle through.

Old Mr. Shakespeare was right. Our lives unfold like one of his famous plays—hopefully with less boredom than high school English classes. Some scenes are full of comedy and joy, while others are full of tragedy. One certainty—people will enter and exit our lives. Some exit because their earthly time is over, others by our own choice. Some people it's like "good riddance," while others leave a deep void of loss. Every person in our life leaves a mark of some kind. Sometimes we have no idea of the impact until suddenly they're gone.

There is an invisible line in time that marks when something changes. We don't see it coming, and there's really no way to prepare for it. We head to work, school, or out to have some fun with expectations and plans that most certainly do not include a life-altering event. Then suddenly, in an instant, everything changes. Life as we know it ceases to exist and will forever be defined by this invisible line of time.

I love to bake, so I like to think that life is a lot like baking. If I use the best ingredients and follow the recipe, things should turn out right. Deep down cognitively, I know better, but it seems like a great concept. After all, who wouldn't want life every day to be like the best batch of chocolate chip cookies ever?

Whatever your philosophy is for life, it generally reflects the idea that we have some sort of control. We need to know that if we check off all the boxes, we can prevent these horrific events. We walk around in our "control bubbles" to create this sense of safety from the hundreds of things that could go wrong every day. If we reflect back to Psychology 101 and Abraham Maslow's hierarchy of needs, we remember that right behind food, water, and shelter, safety is the number one need. We need to feel that we are physically safe from danger as well as emotionally safe with those we trust. It's a defense mechanism. We tell ourselves that tragedy is this awful thing that happens to other people and that somehow, if we just keep the path, we can be insulated from these events. When shocking things happen, we immediately search for a logical answer that fits our model. If my cookies are burned, the oven was too hot, or I left them in too long. There must be an answer. In our minds, nothing just happens without a reason.

A teenager died in a car accident—tragic, but we immediately begin to speculate: *I bet she was drinking, driving recklessly, or not wearing her seatbelt.* The sudden death of a young adult? Yep, they must have been on drugs. Lung cancer? Oh, so sad, but I'm sure they smoked. Our brain desperately needs to make sense of situations and find reasons, because how else will we protect ourselves and our loved ones without this knowledge? The body's number one priority is to survive; therefore, the brain is wired to constantly search for and hold on to negative possibilities.

"Everything happens for a reason." I struggle with this statement. I know people who believe this mantra, and that works for them, but I have a hard time reconciling myself to this sentiment, particularly in the death of children. I have never comforted a grieving parent or thought for one moment that there was a good reason for this event. In those moments, it felt more like "S$%t happens for no reason."

What I have seen more often is people who take events that seem so unreasonable and turn them into projects and programs to help others. A famous example would be John Walsh, the former host of *America's Most Wanted*. He championed the horrific murder of his son Adam into a quest to save other families the pain he and his family endured. Locally, I know a pastor who lost his teenage son and now runs a cutting-edge ministry to help recovering addicts get the fresh start they need to truly stay clean. So yes, on one side there would not be these efforts to help others, but I dare say that each of these men would still prefer to have their children back.

No matter how many people I've sat with through the most unthinkable events— dead children, infidelity, sexual abuse, post war trauma—nothing could have prepared me for the tsunami that was headed my way, nor will anyone convince me that there ever really will be a good reason for it. We can have all the analogies and check all the boxes, but one thing is for sure—once we pass this line, nothing will ever be the same. All the things you think you believe, or didn't believe, will be called into question by yourself and others.

Melissa Collins Harrell

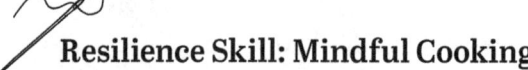
Resilience Skill: Mindful Cooking

Baking or cooking is a great and delicious way to distract yourself when feeling overwhelmed or blue. So many pleasant memories are associated with certain recipes or foods. Either solo or with someone, put on a pot of soup or bake a favorite dessert. Really be present and use your five senses to savor the sights, smells, textures, sounds, and tastes. Reflect on the story behind the recipe and share with others or journal about the memories elicited.

Tapping In

"I am reminded of your sincere faith, a faith that lived first in your grandmother Lois and your mother Eunice and now, I am sure, lives in you"

(2 Timothy 1:5)

NONE OF US WILL escape this life without experiencing the sting of loss. Grief is the deepest pit of human emotion. Finding words to adequately express this level of pain is next to impossible. A broken human heart, no matter the reason, is the worst pain imaginable—a pain so intense that your own mind tries to destroy you. Just like an autoimmune disorder turns the body's defense mechanisms on itself, so the traumatized brain turns on itself until you find yourself fighting for your very life.

The waves come over and over. Some small and tolerable … some more than you can take. Every time you think you're on solid ground, you're knocked back down, sometimes harder than before. Even before these fresh trauma events, I was no stranger to grief. I watched my father wither away and succumb to cancer at age forty-nine. Then I spent the next eleven years caring for my mother as she faded away from mental illness and grief into her early grave at age fifty-two.

One of my best go-to therapy tools is called resourcing. This allows you to tap into a time, place, or person that brings you a sense of peace and safety. It's a foundational skill in managing trauma. We ask our clients to think of a person, place, or memory that brings peace. In the first few days after my life was shattered, I closed my eyes and brought up the image of the small country church I grew up in.

I've never known a life without Jesus. He's the one constant player in my life, another common thread. Growing up in a small rural community, faith has always been an integral part of my life. My faith journey has taken me through the ports of call of Southern Baptist, Lutheran, Catholic, and Methodist. I've also stamped my faith passport with experiences with Jews, Buddhists, Muslims, and many more. As I like to say, when I get to the gates of heaven, I want to ensure that my faith passport is not denied entry, unlike my earthly credit card a few times.

Dissertations and great volumes have been written on the human journey to discover spiritual truth. Believe me, as a hard-core science girl, I know there is absolutely nothing rational about three nails, a cross, and a man rising from the grave, but that's the great mystery of faith. My theology is not complicated. For me, since childhood, it has always been this indescribable longing for a connection beyond myself and a deep desire to serve others. Whatever the faith practices, there are many different threads that run through our lives. Although we may have theological differences, we are all connected by the common threads of wanting to be loved and accepted. In a society that wants us to believe we're so different from one another, we are connected in so many beautiful ways.

We're all pilgrims on a journey to find the meaning and purpose of life. As we travel this path, our threads will intersect and weave in and out of the lives of each other. We're all a part of the fabric of humanity, and as secure of our individuality as we may feel, like it or not, our lives will weave in and out of many people's stories. This will create a complex tapestry containing many juxtaposing experiences: success and disappointments, love and rejection, as well as joy and pain. All these events, positive or difficult, create our personal story and legacy.

My writing has served as a living conversation as I sought to find God and the purpose of my life. Just like any other relationship, this one is a proverbial roller coaster of emotions. In my journaling, every element of my Christian experience is revealed in my own handwriting. My praises, my prayers, my questions, my disappointments, and my ugliest anger are poured out page after page, revealing the relationship and affirmation of the presence of God in my life.

While spending time in Kenya and Guatemala, I felt an instant connection to the women I saw weaving and sewing. Growing up in Western North Carolina, most of my community was employed by the textile industry, and I was surrounded by women with needle and thread in hand. These women created everything from quilts to curtains. I can remember sitting in my great-grandma's house and going through her scrap box. I would pull out random pieces of fabric and wonder why in the world she was keeping these old rags. Undoubtedly, without fail, a few months later she would pull out a finished quilt and, lo and behold, there would be that piece of fabric shining in just the right spot on that quilt. Her artistic eye saw a purpose for every single piece, so nothing was wasted.

My Great Aunt Betty was one of my strongest spiritual mentors and a gifted seamstress. Every year she would deliver a new dress for Easter and Christmas for my sister and myself. She never measured us once, and they fit like a glove. Both of my daughters were baptized in a gorgeous gown she sewed for them. It's one of my most precious treasures.

Ever since the death of my parents, whenever I feel overwhelmed, my heart longs to be near my roots. I guess the more complex life becomes, it's natural to long for the simplicity and familiarity of childhood. I sit down and cover myself with my quilt that is nearing fifty years old. The top is an array of patchwork, and the backing is a soft pink with butterflies. My mom used to lay me on this quilt for tummy time, and she said I would try to catch the butterflies. I run my fingers over the perfectly aligned squares that were tediously hand-stitched one by one and marvel at how the colors and designs differ, yet they all started with the same plain cotton that was then transformed to serve its purpose in the cloth to be designed. How incredible that as different as some things are in other cultures, there are still so many similarities. I am now grounded not only in my own family but feel connected to those women thousands of miles away. I feel embraced and safe.

I recite in my head some positive belief statements. *I can survive this; I am safe. I can get my needs met.* I begin to bring up the image in my mind. I can see the white stone walls and the towering steeple. From my yard as a child, I could see the steeple of my church. It towered high in the sky, and I imagined it was God looking over me. Now in this shadow of the steeple lies the reminder of all of those whom I held so dearly. While not all the influential players in my life are buried there, many are, and like a giant hug, I feel covered and safe by the reminder of their contributions to my life.

A movie reel begins to play out the scenes of my early life. I use my five senses to tap in for the full effect. The memory ribbon unravels and scene after scene begins to flip in my mind, like the view master I used as a child. I see bright red and orange fall foliage, I smell the scent of honeysuckle, I taste fresh baked strawberry pie, I hear the laughter of large family celebrations, and I remember the faces of forgotten friends and favorite dolls. The memories begin to flood over me and, as predicted in my training, I literally feel a physical relaxation in my body.

All my senses are now activated, and I hold my focus on the image of my church. I can feel the hot summer nights of Vacation Bible School, the cool water washing over me on the day of my baptism, the beautiful sounds of a choir singing on Easter Sunday, the feel of a terry cloth bathrobe I wore in Christmas plays, heartfelt altar calls for forgiveness, and the heart flutters of a first crush.

I bask in the relief of release that flows through my body, which has been running in fight or flight for days now. I am mentally and physically drained and yearn for the switch to turn this all off. There is nothing left to give. In this quiet space, there is no expectation of me. I don't have to figure this all out. I find relief and temporary shelter from the fear and suffocating pain.

I continue to breathe in deeply and soak up my memories. In the middle of these beautiful thoughts, there begins an intrusion. Other memories arise—ones that do not bring me peace. They hold deep sadness and pain. I sense the tensing of my once relaxed body and feel the tears begin to flow.

My memories are no longer peaceful and safe. The trauma memory chain begins, and like a line of dominoes they flow without warning. The smell of rubbing alcohol permeates, and I am in a hospital room sharing Cheetos with my dad while a bag of experimental chemo drips into his body. Next, I am locking tearful eyes with him on my wedding day and giving thanks because he made it to give me away. A few weeks later, I'm hugging his cancer-ridden body for the last time on Thanksgiving Day. As this thread ends, I see myself placing one last kiss on his forehead before his casket is closed for the final time.

The tears are overwhelming, and the sobs are now audible as the scene quickly shifts. I'm having a conversation with my mom and longing for the mom who raised me, not this mentally ill version I no longer know. My body flinches as I remember the click of the doors locking behind me as I walk out of a behavioral health unit while she begs me not to leave her. I'm flooded with feelings of helplessness and guilt, and my hands tingle as I remember the simultaneous rush of pain and relief that came the night I found out she had died.

I quickly open my eyes and reorient myself to the room. This is not good. I recognize that not only am I reeling from my current crisis, but all my past trauma threads are also unraveling. I know that I'm in very dangerous waters. I am not safe. It's time to return to therapy.

Resilience Skill: Resourcing

Find a location where you feel safe and comfortable, free of distractions. Turn off as many noises as possible.

Sit or lie in a comfortable position. You can sit in a chair with your feet in contact with the earth, sit on the floor, or lie on your back.

Begin by turning your attention to your breath and taking deep breaths.

Begin to notice any sensations in your body: tightness, discomfort, tingles, pain.

Visualize the breath traveling into each area and release these areas on the exhale.

Bring up the image you want to focus on. It can be a person, place, animal. Use your five senses to explore the sights, sounds, smells, touch, and taste that would be associated with this resource.

Before returning to your space, take three slow, deep breaths to seal in your peace.

Responsibility

Begin at the Beginning

"'Begin at the beginning,' the King said, very gravely, 'and go on till you come to the end: then stop.'"

—Lewis Carroll, *Alice in Wonderland*

MY THERAPIST, ANNA'S, OFFICE is a safe space for me. I'm in desperate need of this space today as I'm actively in Acute Stress Disorder. My body has been running for days in fight or flight mode. I can't eat, and when I'm forced to by friends, my lovely nemesis, IBS, ensures that it doesn't last long. Sleep is elusive, and forget trying to concentrate. I am constantly startled by every unexpected noise. In mental health, we refer to this as a state of hypervigilance. My brain is on high alert for the next stressor. I'm haunted with flashbacks of that day, and phrases keep floating through my head. Nothing feels safe.

Although I crave the safety that Anna's office provides for me in this storm, entering her office again feels so defeating. After all, I'd already done this therapy thing, and I was supposed to be healed and out there living my best life. Even though rationally I know there are no limits to the curves life can throw you, I still unconsciously believed there was a formula. After all the battles with family mental illness, losing my parents so early, and years of walking through the wilderness to find the path God was calling me to, I erroneously believed that I had been through my fair share of tests. I mean, come on, I had traveled to Kenya and Guatemala to do the Lord's work. Doesn't being willing to go to places I never wanted to go give me some bonus points?

We don't want to admit it, but deep down we all know. You can do it all right, the best you know how, and still have a kid who struggles with addiction, a broken marriage, or a failed business. It's a bit like getting on the boat to ride "It's a Small Word" only to find yourself in the "Haunted Mansion" a few more times than planned.

Anna is a seasoned therapist, which she would tell you means old, but I'd say that means that she had been around this therapy block a time or two. I began working with her in 2015 to deal with my secondary compassion fatigue and emerging midlife career crisis. She was the perfect match for me. I didn't need some fresh-out-of-school save-the-world Barbie. No, I needed a Rambo therapist, someone who knew life would chew you up and spit you out a few times. We have a very good therapeutic arrangement. She gives me therapy, and along with my copay each session, I bring her some comedic relief. What can I say? Humor has always been my go-to coping skill; I learned it from my dad.

One of the frustrations of mental health work is that we have no X-rays or diagnostic tests to guide us. Using instinct, empathy, and an insane amount of education that we will spend the rest of our lives paying back, we stumble through this darkness alongside our client. Along the journey, we are unaware of the amount of transference that is occurring as we share space with client after client. No matter how much high-level training or experience you master, at the end of the day, you are human.

You never get immune to the gut-wrenching cries of a mother who didn't get to bring her baby home, the innocent survivor of sexual abuse, or the soldier who still believes twenty years later he could have saved his best friend. In fact, I don't want to know the person who could get used to that level of exposure to raw human pain.

Prior to working with Anna, I remember lying in bed one night with tears flowing nonstop and just repeating over and over, "I'm so broken." I was so angry at myself for allowing myself to be so weak, and I was disappointed that I hadn't seen this coming. I mean, after all, I am a Type A super planner, and I didn't write "Have a breakdown" on my calendar. Salt to the wound, I was a frequent speaker at many women's groups, where I advocated for them to practice better self-care. In essence, this felt like I was an epic failure at practicing what I preach, and I was embarrassed.

That's the scary thing with compassion fatigue or burnout: it's a lot like beach erosion. You can't see the way your work is changing you every day. All the empathy, hope, and compassion that is filling the life of others is slowly taking pieces of you away. Viewed in a time lapse, the changes would appear drastic. I was a shell of my former self. After years of helping guide others out of the darkness, my own inner light was slowly being extinguished. I was barely keeping my head above the water. I decided something had to change. I finally had to admit that I needed professional help. Admitting that the very work that broke me was what I needed to heal me was a hard pill to swallow.

Entering her office five years ago for my initial session, I felt that this could be wrapped up in eight to twelve solution-focused sessions. Hand over the pad, lady, and just let me write out this treatment plan. A little cognitive behavioral for the depression, some career development, some stress coping tools, and we should be good to go. Of course, things on paper always look much easier than the true state of the human heart. As I stated earlier, the problems that bring a person into therapy are just symptoms but not the root of all their pain.

By the time people usually come in for therapy, they're in crisis, and they want immediate relief from the situation. I was no different and was ready for immediate relief. The issue they seek resolution and relief from is certainly happening in the present, but what we don't realize is that we're all operating from a core set of beliefs. These beliefs and neurological pathways were formed in early childhood long before this moment and have been reinforced over time. We're learning so much about the impact and how that shapes us and what factors increase resilience. The one truth we know is that if you want to change who you are now, you have to look at the root, where it all started, and that is not today.

In my graduate counseling program, it was highly suggested that we attend therapy before graduation, but it wasn't a requirement. Well, it wasn't required, and I was busy. What started out as a journey to address my compassion fatigue, emerging midlife identity crisis, and depression over being depressed began to unravel my deep trauma roots. I could no longer hide behind my tough "save the world' exterior. I had met my match, and she saw right through my BS!

In this space I was finally forced to acknowledge myself as the little girl who had been allowed to assume responsibility for taking care of others way before her time. To shield myself from these overwhelming tasks, I had created core beliefs about myself. My motto had become "My pain and needs are secondary to the needs of others," and I was "the strong one." I was the family rescuer and fixer. Mix that in with a heaping dose of the following labels to be reinforced—Southern, Christian, female—and you have what we so affectionately refer to now as a "hot mess."

What a relief to finally verbalize the annoyance, the rage, and the absolute unfairness I felt of having to take care of all the people in my family over the years who struggled with mental illness. Especially the burden of helping to caretake for others halfway across the state while being a working mom with three young children.

Today is different. I sit before her in the biggest crisis of my life, along with a complex trauma history. Hey, go big or go home, right? Our previous sessions together were very solution focused, and while they did touch on my past, I know this trauma would open again my entire past. I would need to dig deeper than ever in my life to survive this, and I wasn't sure if I had any fight left. Yes, I have survived 100 percent of my past pains, but what if this is the one time that I can't come back?

My brain looped negative thought after negative thought. What will happen when all the Band Aids I've so skillfully applied to avoid releasing the pain over the years come flying off? My stomach was in knots. Could I survive the bleeding and surge of pain while I was already so bruised and battered? Maybe this was my cat life number ten and would finally finish me off. Was it too late to choose sedation first?

The trust between a therapist and client is a very sacred bond. I anxiously looked at Anna as if she had a magic answer to make this all go away. She paused to acknowledge the heaviness of this situation and then asked, "What is the most distressing thing to you right now?"

Hot tears flowed nonstop as I answered. "The overwhelming sense of responsibility, that everything is all on me. I have three humans who are counting on me for everything, and that weight is crushing. I feel like I've fought so hard to get to a better place, and here I am right back in the same place—overwhelmed, alone, and responsible for everyone and everything. "

Anna settled back into her chair. "Tell me the first time you remember feeling responsible for everyone?"

Melissa Collins Harrell

Resilience Skill: Journal

Write about your life experiences with responsibility. Do you take on more than your share? Where do you need to let go and accept what you're responsible for? What are some actions you can take today, tomorrow, next week to make this happen?

Running from Insanity

"Sickness, insanity and death were the angels that surrounded my cradle and they have followed me throughout my life."

—Edvard Munch

ANYONE WHO KNOWS ME knows that I'm a self-proclaimed "non-runner." I hang out with runners. I own runner shoes and gear, but I do not run. However, given my family history, I feel like I've literally been running from insanity my entire life. In the South, the consensus is that we don't ask if you have crazy people in your family. We ask what side they're on. Well, lucky for me, that would be both. In a clinical interview we explore family history of mental health and substance abuse issues. Mine looks something like this:

Father's Side: ADHD, Generalized Anxiety Disorder, Schizophrenia, OCD, alcoholism, PTSD

Mother's Side: Bipolar Disorder times three, suicide attempts, addiction, PTSD

My hope had always been that just like two negatives make a positive, the two sides would clash into one big cloud of sanity.

Even early on as a professional counselor with the ability to assess trauma, I didn't believe that I had experienced any childhood trauma. My childhood was magical to me. As a child, it all seemed normal and wonderful, but then again, I didn't know that life could look any other way. As an adult with a counseling degree, it would take me years to process the impact that growing up in a family with mental illness had on me.

I love rural North Carolina, and I have a deep passion for the people and places of my home state. I believe you can have pageant tiaras and advanced degrees in the same trophy case. I can equally enjoy a fascinating conversation with the governor or the farmer down the street. My accent represents a heritage rather than my IQ, and I wear my hillbilly roots with pride.

Growing up in the foothills of North Carolina in the 1980s was, in my biased opinion, exceptional. Like many Southern kids, I was surrounded by an array of family that made sure I was loved, looked after, and disciplined as needed. Every single home on either side of us up and down the winding country road housed a relative.

My life from birth was touched by mental illness, again something I just thought was normal in every family. My parents beat the odds of teen pregnancy and the edge of poverty to rise from a single wide trailer to home ownership. I was the first four-year college graduate in my family. While I always valued this, now as a therapist and social justice advocate, I know just what a gift this is.

I'm not sure why in the world I would expect a linear path in this life, seeing as I came into the world unexpectedly. I've always hated the term "unplanned pregnancy" because, get real, for the most part the majority of us aren't planned by our parents. My mom was only sixteen when she became pregnant with me, and my parents married in November of 1972, before I was born in May of 1973. I can't remember how old I was before I knew it took a baby nine months to grow and mentally did the math to realize I had a front row seat at my parents' wedding. I may have been unexpected, and my parents were young, but I was never unwanted. Even though I always felt loved and wanted, knowing that my mom and dad's life plan was guided by my existence was a burden that I carried. Deep down, I always wanted to let them know that I was worth it, that they'd made the right choice and their sacrifices weren't wasted. As a child, it felt like the least I could do, but now as a parent myself, it seems ridiculous.

After my birth, my parents set up their single wide trailer on "the hill," as it became referred to in our lives. My dad's mom, Velma, or Granny, as I called her, lived next door to us. My mom with rolling eyes recounted the story over and over how Granny would come and sit on a log outside my bedroom window for hours every day while I napped. Now before you think she was the sweetest grandmother in the world, you should know her true motive: she didn't trust my mom to hear me cry.

Like most kids of my day, I didn't attend preschool, so she was my caregiver while my parents worked. She loved me dearly and took excellent care of me. She taught me how to sew and make paper dolls. She encouraged me in all my endeavors, and I do mean all. She listened to me practice the same piano songs over and over. Honest, I don't know how she could stand it. I hit enough wrong notes hours on end to make a terrorist talk.

All these sound like typical grandmother qualities, but Granny was anything but typical. She suffered from probably one of the most misunderstood mental health diagnoses: paranoid schizophrenia. This disorder affects a person's ability to think, feel, and behave and causes them to lose touch with reality. Her mentally ill brain caused her to pace the floors constantly and talk to dead people. Seriously, the woman wore out shoes like a NASCAR driver burns tires.

In the 1970s, the treatments and stigma related to mental health were far from where we are today. Psychiatric care opportunities were few and far between, especially in rural areas, and what did exist was cold and archaic at best. Most of her life, Granny had no psychiatric care. Once my mom began her nursing studies, she tried to get my dad to take her to a psychiatrist, but he would have no part of it. Granny did have one stay in Broughton Hospital, one of our state facilities. According to family legend, Velma left, took a taxi home, looked at a family member, and said, "Pay the man." For the record, that's an eighty-mile one way trip from Morganton, North Carolina to Elkin. You do the math.

In between our daily tender interactions, she would pace and get into serious arguments with her dead brothers and other people who'd died long before my arrival. These rants were woven with a string of profanity that would make a sailor blush. I never remember feeling unsafe or afraid of her, and obviously my parents never thought she would harm me. Of course, in her stable mind she wouldn't, but as a clinician now, I count myself fortunate that she never had a significant break in my presence. Once the brain entered a stage of psychotic break, she could have viewed me as her dead brother or a person out to harm her, and things could have turned into a crisis very quickly. At age five, the only details I knew about Granny's brother, my Great Uncle Rich, I learned listening to her rages. If someone had asked me to tell them about Great Uncle Rich, I would have said with the innocent face of a five-year-old, "Oh, he's that mean SOB that took my granny's money. "

Groceries and Throw Downs

IF EVER ANYONE REFLECTED the term "moxie," it was Velma. I mean, there's nothing like a delusional person to show you what it means to not give a rat's ass what other people think about you. For most of my childhood, I just thought everyone's grandparents talked to dead people. What's incredible about the schizophrenic brain is that she could be completely engrossed in deep conversation with one of these apparitions, and I could say, "Granny, I want some apple juice," she would stop, retrieve my juice, and then immediately light back into her rage.

On top of her mental health issues, she was a type 1 diabetic who, due to paranoia, refused to believe the doctor. They were all liars out to kill her, and she wasn't taking those shots. Some kids watched cartoons while they ate their morning cereal before heading off to school. My morning entertainment, which upon reflection did resemble an episode of *Tom and Jerry*, was to watch my dad run around the house attempting to give her the daily insulin shot.

Because I was so close to her, I was one of the only people who could get her to do things she needed to do. It was always the same story. The weekly grocery store trip looked something like this: My dad and Granny argued on the way to the store about why she insisted on shopping at the most expensive store in town. Then, by aisle three, my dad and Granny would be in a shouting match. He'd retreat to the car, and I'd be left to navigate the rest of the store experience.

Let me tell you, navigating a grocery store with a type 1 diabetic in denial is a real joy. The cart was loaded with cookies, jelly rolls, and Dr. Pepper. When she wasn't looking, to help her out, I would toss things I knew she didn't need back on the shelves. I don't think she appreciated my attempts to be a diabetic nutritionist at age ten. One day as we made our way down the milk aisle, she finally got wise to my tricks. When she investigated the contents of her cart and saw her sugary items removed, I caught a line of profanity and anger just like Uncle Rich!

Moxie Meets Kevin

AS THE YEARS ROLLED on, the dysfunctional dance continued and I became comfortable in this role of peacekeeper between my dad and Granny. This also began to support the core belief that I was responsible for people. This dysfunction also became my superpower. I was a helper, and I was good at it. Show me someone in a uniform or helping career, and I can almost guarantee you a trauma history. It's a part of our identity; it's just what we do.

In high school, like most girls, I experienced my fair shares of crushes. One of those boys was an upperclassman named Kevin, and he happened to work at the high-end grocery store that Granny won the weekly battle to shop at. Each week the opportunity to see him while enduring the grocery battles made it worth my while. I can assure you there were large volumes of Rave hairspray and roll-on cherry flavored lip gloss involved.

One week Granny was all obsessed with finding this spice named "Sicily." I was like, "Granny, Sicily is a place, not a spice. I think you want Italian seasoning." Nope, she told me she knew good and damn well that was a spice. Oh, but yes, as this argument continued and her squeaky grocery cart rolled into the spice aisle. Yep, you guessed it—there stood Kevin stocking the spice aisle.

Oh God, I just wanted to die right there. Here we go. Granny asked him for this fictitious spice, while all along I stood behind her waving my arms like someone trying to be rescued from a deserted island, mouthing, "She's crazy; just tell her you don't have it." He was very courteous and said that they didn't carry that. How I wish that was the end of that story, but she proceeded to call him a liar and marched to the back of the store into the storeroom to look for herself. Needless to say, Kevin never asked me out.

A Call for Healing

"Being heard is so close to being loved that for the average person, they are almost indistinguishable."

—David W. Augsburger

I WASN'T THE ONLY unplanned pregnancy in my family. My granny was an unwed mother in the 1940s. She became pregnant while working in another state and returned to our community with a small child, my dad. There are varying accounts of what happened, and the truth lies buried with her. Whether it was consensual or not, one thing is for sure—she didn't plan on becoming a mother at that stage of her life.

It pains my heart to know how my granny suffered and was stigmatized after the birth of my father in 1948. This trauma likely contributed to the unraveling of her lifetime battle with depression and schizophrenia. Though many mysteries still surround schizophrenia, there are theories that the gene is passed on and that traumatic events can awaken the disease. My cousin shared with me that she used to see my granny sitting on the porch and rocking my dad while she cried uncontrollably. As someone who suffered from postpartum depression, that image haunts me. I can't imagine that depth of pain in a time when no one understood how to help.

No one probably ever told her, but my granny never felt like she could go back to church after my dad was born. She carried the shame of being an unwed mother in her body like an invisible scarlet letter. I never saw her attend church, but her faith was undeniable. In between her breaks from reality, she walked around singing hymns and encouraged me to recite Bible verses to her. Years later, I discovered that she had written several songs, some of them hymns. She even attempted to get them published. I guess the writing root runs deep.

I wonder what her life would have been like with proper treatment for her trauma and schizophrenia. Maybe she would have been less anxious to drive, and we could have had grand adventures. Possibly she could have felt safe enough to meet another man and forge a happy relationship. Treatment for her condition in the early years would have also greatly impacted my dad, allowing him to grow up exposed to less anxiety and adversity due to poverty. Sadly, these things didn't occur, and my granny lived her life locked in a prison within her own brain. What talent the world never saw in her music and her spirit, all because the world judged her based on one act in her life—an act in which she possibly had no voice. There was never any conversation about the man, and to my knowledge no one knows who he was, at least no one left alive. I imagine his life went on without missing a beat.

Trauma can also be inflicted by cultural standards. It's appalling to me the way women can be shunned and treated "less than," as if they impregnated themselves. Sadly, this mentality still holds true in many places. Knowing my family history has fueled my work with girls all over the world. Access to accurate women's health education and birth control are great equalizers for women. What a difference every generation of women makes for the next through education.

We also must do some serious work in our churches. Living in the South, our churches have been and continue to be hubs of our community. Sadly, so often even lifelong Christians feel judged and too ashamed to turn to their religious homes for support through the most difficult situations. I hope we can get to the place where other struggles like addiction, sexual struggles, and mental illness feel welcomed in the church. The church should be a sanctuary where people feel loved and supported regarding their mental health. Rather than feeling ashamed of taking psychiatric medication, or made to feel spiritually weak for seeking counseling, they should be supported and encouraged there. We're all broken, and of all places, the church should be a place where we can be open, share our brokenness, and strive to heal together.

Resilience Skill: Support Groups

Connecting with others who are struggling with similar issues such as grief, addiction, illness, and divorce can be very powerful. Check online as well. Even though in person is wonderful, online can also offer powerful support.

Caregiving Gene

"It's not the load that breaks you down. It's the way you carry it."

—Lena Horne

AFTER GRANNY'S SLOW DECLINE with dementia, which is more common in people who suffer from schizophrenia, my dad made the difficult decision to place her in a nursing facility. While this is never an easy decision for anyone, we are conditioned from birth in the South that putting people in a nursing home is what bad kids do to their parents. There are so many emotions related to caregiving, but the number one by far has to be guilt. This guilt monster is often fed by a steady diet of "should," "oughts," and "musts" that have been ingrained in our brains as truths for most of our lives. These thoughts lead us to unhelpful messages, such as: I "ought" to take care of my dad at home; I "should" spend more time with my mom; and I "must" never lose my patience with my loved one. These self-judgments that we hear in our heads just add to the guilt and heartache that one already naturally faces in these moments.

Once Granny went into a nursing facility, my dad would bring her home on the weekends to do her laundry and have visits. When I was able, I would ride with him on the thirty-minute commute to pick her up and bring her home to visit for the day. My mom never understood my dad's need to do this every weekend, but I know it was to relieve the guilt he felt in not being able to care for her at home. On one occasion after being picked up, she looked at my dad with sincerity and said, "Phillip, did you know that my brother Rich died?" To which my dad replied to her with profound joy, "Praise God, Rich is dead!" This joy was fueled by the fact that he knew her mentally ill brain now grasped that her brother was truly dead. Now that he was gone from her mind, we would never have to hear her talk about him ever again. True to the schizophrenic brain, that was the last we ever heard of Uncle Rich. Finally, poor man, his soul can rest in peace.

Watching someone fade away into dementia is torture, but God gave me a sweet closure with my granny. I was home from college on a break, and I knew that her time left here was growing short. When I arrived, I brought her a vanilla ice cream, her favorite treat. As we sat enjoying our ice cream, I felt so frustrated that she didn't even remember me. At one point, I was one of the most precious people to her, and now in this moment I was no more than a stranger. She asked me questions that you would ask someone you just met in the grocery story. I was so angry at God for all this pain in her life. She hadn't only experienced such hardship, but she never achieved her own personal dreams, and in the end, she knew none of the people whom she loved. Really, what kind of God allows this?

I grabbed my coat and bent down to kiss her, and as I turned to walk out the door, she sat up in her bed and called my full name: "Melissa Suzanne."

I turned back to her in great surprise.

"I'll miss you when I'm gone."

I ran back in and hugged her, etching every touch into my memory, knowing that would be the last one. A few days later, after I had returned to school, I received the call that she had died peacefully in her sleep. I could just envision her crossing the heavenly finish line as her earthly mental shackles fell away. Schizophrenia and shame are not welcome here in her eternal home. For once, she was loved and accepted unconditionally and was finally at peace.

The Invisible Workforce

CAREGIVERS ARE OFTEN CALLED the invisible workforce. They're like angels all around us as childcare workers, home health aides, and family members who are taking care of young children, the sick, disabled, and ageing. They are undervalued and grossly underpaid in our country. While like my dad, there are men who are caregivers, this workforce is overwhelmingly made up of women and an overwhelming number are women of color. My maternal grandma was a certified nursing assistant, and my mom was a registered nurse, so caregiving runs deep in our veins. In addition to caregiving on the job, these women were also a large part of the invisible workforce as they cared for various family members over the years.

One perk of having a young mother is also having a young grandmother. My Grandma Maxine, or Lean Mean Maxine, as I called her, was only thirty-two years old when I was born. I know, crazy. I was that age when my youngest child was born. Back in the day when medical care wasn't so dominated by lawsuits and there was no such thing as HIPPA, the federal law that protects patients' confidentiality, I spent many a day following my grandma around while she worked at a local nursing home. I watched her while she bathed, dressed, and showered the residents with love. It was simultaneously ordinary and lovely for me to watch her work. Because of her beautiful example, I have never known any other way than to treat people with great love and dignity. I attribute the fact that I'm a mental health therapist to my grandma. She was always bragging about the benefits of therapy, and she bought me a complete set of books on feelings that I read over and over, which likely sharpened the social and emotional area of my brain.

Over the years, my grandma's deep love and compassion, no doubt coupled with some good old Southern woman guilt, led her to become a primary caregiver at home to multiple relatives. She would take care of them around the clock until they required a level of care she could no longer provide. The financial impacts on caregivers are incredible. Caring for family members causes many women to have to reduce the number of hours they work, take a leave of absence, or make other career changes. All the hours that are spent caring for children or relatives are hours they could have been at a paying job and earning towards retirement benefits—yet more reasons why so many more women fall into poverty than men.

This caregiving model hit even closer to home when our dad was diagnosed with colon cancer at the young age forty-seven. I watched my mom commit to the ultimate nursing shifts as she cared for our dad at home as he battled cancer until his last breath. Caregiver syndrome, or caregiver stress, is a real condition. It often manifests with symptoms of exhaustion, anger, rage, or guilt. The physical and emotional tolls of extended caregiving are astounding. Family caregivers are more likely to experience negative health effects such as depression, anxiety, and even chronic disease themselves. Caregiving for long periods of time puts the body under chronic stress, which has been shown to cause change and damage at the cellular level. This type of caregiving is draining enough on healthy people but beyond not ideal for someone on disability herself for bipolar disorder. This was a very serious crisis unfolding.

So there we were. My sister was barely out of high school with a young child, and I was newly married, working, and in graduate school. At a time in our lives when our parents would normally be helping us launch out into the world with whatever supports, emotional and financial, they could, we were left trying to figure out how best to support our parents. We were dealing with all ends of the spectrum—a stubborn dad who insisted on taking chemo and going to work, and a mom whose moods were beyond unpredictable.

Anticipatory grief reactions are the grief symptoms that occur before the physical death of a loved one, sometimes referred to as "the long goodbye." This is most often associated with dementia or Alzheimer's diagnosis but really goes along with many mental health issues or a terminal diagnosis. So many losses are associated with these diseases, such as grief associated with the loss of the health of your loved one and the loss of the life you knew with this person. We had this going on with both of our parents simultaneously—slowly watching our dad's physical body wither away to cancer while watching an invisible cancer of sorts erode our mom's brain.

The Mother Load

"If it's not one thing it's your mother."

—Robin Williams

AFTER OUR DAD SURRENDERED his battle to cancer in 1997, my sister and I shared in caretaking of our mom with bipolar disorder. At the time of his death, our mom was only forty-one, on disability, and experiencing a revolving door of multiple admissions to psychiatric facilities. Loving someone with mental illness is full of more emotions than can be typed on these pages. While I treasure many photos of me with my mom, there is one very special one. I'm less than six months old, and she is bathing me. This picture captures perfectly the mother-baby eye gaze connection. You can see that the souls have connected, and we're both smiling because we feel the love. While this photo is precious, as a mental health practitioner I know that attachment was key to my development.

When I was five years old, what I considered at that time to be a traumatic event occurred—my baby sister was born. This was a shattering event for me, not because I wanted to be an only child, but because I had ordered a baby brother whose name was supposed to be Jamie. Instead, I got a baby sister named Amy. All of this caused me to be quite upset, so when she arrived home from the hospital, this drama queen was not enjoying all the attention the little princess was receiving.

There was nothing left to do but defend my title, and it started with taking back my rightful throne—the crib. The look on my mom's face when she realized that a five-year-old had skillfully climbed into the crib, removed her sleeping newborn sister, and placed herself in the crib did not result in the royal fanfare I had hoped for. I don't really remember what she said; I just remembered that I decided I had to run away. So I packed all my childhood belongings (ok, only a few toys and stuffed animals) into my red plastic suitcase that read "I'm going to Grandmas." I picked up my suitcase, said my goodbyes, and ran all the way next door to Granny's house.

What I couldn't have known as a young child but learned later was that my struggles and challenges adjusting to becoming a big sister paled in comparison to what my mom was going through with postpartum depression (PPD). Years later, I would gain a new understanding of PPD after the birth of my third child.

While having three kids in three-and-a-half years should have been a warning flag that I was at risk for PPD, there were other ones, such as my Type A perfectionistic personality. However, what was an even bigger clue was that my mom and my sister had both suffered from PPD. I had amazing midwives and supportive providers, but very few people were talking about PPD or doing universal screenings of new moms in the early 2000s when I was having babies. For the first few months after my son's birth, I felt great. In fact, I was slightly confident that I had found some sort of rhythm in all the madness of three kids under age four. Giving birth, I was a warrior, and that moment made me believe that if I could get through childbirth, I could get through anything. Man, denial is a beast.

When I wasn't at home running what looked like my own childcare business, I was working in private practice. Every day as a routine part of my job, I was assessing clients for depression and anxiety. During these screenings, it never occurred to me that I was not myself. As the months went on, I began to sense that something wasn't right, but being a driven professional, I was not going to let this "whatever feeling" win.

I was also secretly petrified that if I admitted to being clinically depressed, I'd begin to spiral into a place of no return, just like my mother. Part of my fear with admitting that I was depressed was that this was the start of a spiral of mental health issues that would destroy not only my life but my family. While my mom's PPD didn't cause her to develop bipolar disorder, it was a prequel of what was to come. For years I had worried that just like a cancer gene lying dormant, I would wake up one day and find myself diagnosed with bipolar disorder. Nope ... I was totally "fine." Just sleep deprived.

No one knew because on the exterior, I was thriving. I was taking great care of my kids, going on dates with my husband, calling friends, and working hard at my career. When I went in to see health care professionals for myself or the kids, I'd report that I was doing great. Finally, one day I was all out of pretend energy and I broke down with my husband. I admitted I wasn't fine, far from it, and once the tears were allowed to come, I thought they would never stop.

In 2006, living in a rural community, I had to travel over forty-five miles one way to access care, which included therapy, medication, and a support group. All of these supports together helped me to heal and restore my soul. This opened a season of beautiful work in my life. I was blessed to have great support and the resources to access help, but what about the women who didn't have the time or resources to drive all this way? I believed these resources should be everywhere. It then became my mission that no mother in our area should have to do this alone. My collaborative work with other community advocates to bring mental health support to pregnant and postpartum mothers will always be some of the most important work that I ever do—work that I would have never been as empathetic for or truly understood were it not for my personal battles. I am incredibly proud of the strides we've made over the last few decades in our community and internationally to help support mothers and families to access adequate care and recovery.

In January of 2006, I wrote this letter to my daughters in their baby journals because I know that the thread for PPD is there, and awareness is everything.

Dear Daughter,

This is for you to read one day when you are all grown up and have a family of your own. As hard as it is for me to believe looking at your tiny face now, you will likely be a mom someday. I know as you read through this journal it sounds as if every day was happy, but being a parent is tough. I just want you to know that there were also plenty of days of frustration, anger, tears, and deep depression. Never be afraid to admit to these struggles or reach out for help. I hope I will be around to help you. Love, Mom

If you or someone you know are struggling to adjust to motherhood, please visit Post-Partum Support International at psi.net for resources to help.

Unexpected Gifts

"Mayhem and chaos don't toughen you up, and they don't prepare you well to deal with the terror of this world. Tender love and care toughen you up, because they nurture and strengthen your capacity to learn and adapt—including learning how to fight and adapting to later hardship."

—Noam Shpancer, PhD:

AS MY MOM'S BATTLE with bipolar disorder raged over the years, it eroded her sense of self-esteem as well as her hope in the world. Our once vibrant mother who tackled nursing school with honors while raising two children barely had the confidence to get dressed some days. Just like Alzheimer's eats away at the person we know and leaves a shell, so can many other mental health issues. Unfortunately for me and my sister, we were also the ones on the receiving end of many hurtful comments, negative letters, and heartbreaking events. Due to her mental illness, our mom died to us years before her physical body left this earth. After her death, one of the hardest things I did was walk all my mom's journals straight out to a dumpster. The mental health counselor and writer wanted to understand her journey, but the daughter knew there would be things written in various states of mind that would cut me to the core and haunt me forever.

These are the times when I drew on that image of the photo of me and my mom. It was important for me to remember that connection because years later, looking in her eyes felt like looking at a stranger. My mom's illness could take me in a day from one end of the emotional spectrum to another. I could talk with her in the morning and be so frustrated because she wouldn't follow through with simple tasks, yet later that day, I'd find myself tearful in grief over the loss of my mom. One week I could get a card in the mailbox telling me how proud she was, and the next week I'd receive a five-page letter stating that I was the reason she never fulfilled any of her dreams. When you live with a parent with mental illness, you learn early on to get some thick skin.

In 2006, I threw a surprise party for my mom for her fiftieth birthday. I had no idea that two short years later she would be gone forever or that the special gift I gave her would become one of my greatest treasures. I've always been a sucker for a Hallmark gimmick, but this one really spoke to me. It was a memory book in which people wrote letters to the birthday person. I mailed out the letters with the instructions to many of her friends and family and waited for their arrivals. One by one as these letters were mailed back to me, I placed them in the book.

As I placed these letters in her book, an unexpected thing began to happen for me: my mom's life story came alive. I read as her close friend Brenda talked about how my mom knocked on her door one day and asked if she'd like to get together and let their girls play. This was the beginning of not only their friendship but a now forty-five-year friendship with my cradle baby friend, Misty. My mom and Brenda also dreamed together about going back to school, my mom for nursing and Brenda for teaching.

This was beyond a bold move for two working moms in the early 1980s. They signed up for classes at the local community college and commuted together, each supporting and finally achieving their dreams. Letter after letter affirmed my mom's tenacity for getting through RN school with two kids and running a household. My mom was actually told by one community college advisor that she should go home and take care of her family, as there was no way she could handle nursing school and young children. Her response to that was to choose a different school and graduate top of her class. I guess persistence is hereditary.

So many letters complimented her on her smile and her willingness to go the extra mile to help anyone in need. Apparently my mom had also been holding back a big secret: she was a community hero. After destroying the one-lane bridge at Long Branch Creek in her Grand Torino, a new wider, two-lane bridge was constructed. According to my cousin Vance in his letter: "Years later, the community is still enjoying it." Reading through these stories just illustrated the threads of community and support. All these backstories and underlying subplots under the surface are so important, but we never see them. I'm so glad she was able to read these letters while she was still alive.

Not only did my sister and I have the tremendous caregiving responsibilities of my mom and our Grandma Maxine, but we also lacked active grandparents to support us with young children. I was often envious of the support and relationships my peers shared with their parents. Loss upon loss, as I would say to a client. My grandma had also struggled with mental health issues her entire life, with multiple hospitalizations for major depressive disorder that was finally properly diagnosed as bipolar disorder a few short years before her death. For several years she and my mom lived together, but due to a rapid onset of Alzheimer's, my sister finally had to move her to a facility near her.

Our mom and grandma died less than five months apart. Mom had a massive heart attack, and Grandma succumbed to Alzheimer's complications. Although the true mom my sister and I knew had died years before, her physical death at age fifty-two was still sudden and quite shocking. Knowing the way that she died was also heavy and extremely hard to process as her child. Our mom lived alone and would go days or weeks without contacting anyone due to her mood shifts, including her daughters. She was also notorious for not answering her phone if you called, and we'd been doing this dance for over ten years. Even though we knew that we couldn't have prevented her death, to know that she lay dead after her heart attack for several days before she was found was a horrific thought. To think about how I was going about my day for several days while she was dead, and that no one knew … the weight of that guilt and sadness can't ever be fully expressed.

This weight of caregiving placed an incredible physical, emotional, and financial strain on both me, my sister, and our husbands. As is so often the case in these difficult situations, family members find themselves in direct conflict with the very people they should turn to for support and strength. This is precisely what happened with me and my sister. While we've both always been strong willed and stubborn, adding these impossible levels of stress, along with differences in opinions on care, created scars that sadly still impact our relationship today.

All through these years, I was trying to mother three small children, be a wife, and build my career. While it's the circle of life to take care of your parents, this just seemed too early and a huge burden to handle all at once. I felt so guilty for feeling angry and resentful for the time that was taken from my family, and my mental and physical health were being impacted. So while their deaths were too early and still pierce me with waves of sadness, there was also an incredible relief to release all those caregiving duties. I could finally focus on my current responsibilities and not live in fear of how the next phone call would dictate my day or weeks to come.

These midlife years and raising teens have brought many challenges for me, and how I long for the mom that held me so safely in that baby photo. To call her and hear her say "Hang in there," or just to hear that someone over eighteen thinks I'm doing a good job. To ask her advice: "Hey, this is what I'm thinking about doing. What do you think?" To text her and share how her grandchild did the kindest thing. Greater still, to sit with her over a cup of coffee and apologize for being a know it all sixteen-year-old who now knows that she knew absolutely nothing. And to give her that greatest piece of information ever: Her wish has been granted. I have a child just like me!

Today I sit alone with my cup of coffee during this most unimaginable crisis. The little girl in me longs for her mom more than ever. Once I married, the one stable source of support in my life was filled by my husband. He was who I turned to for support when everything else was falling apart. He was it; I had no one else. Now here I am, alone, with the weight of the world on me, and my deepest fear, failure, clawing like wolves at every door and window of my house, trying to get in and eat me up.

Resilience Skill: Create a Self-Care Menu

Using a sheet, make a space for each of these: 1 min, 5 mins, 15 mins, 30 mins , 1 hour, half a day, 1 day, 1 week. List something you could do within these minutes to take care of yourself. Here are some jump starters.

1 minute = Keep a favorite lotion nearby. Slowly apply and inhale deeply.

5 minutes = Close your eyes and do a mediation.

15 minutes = Take a bath.

30 minutes = Take a mindful nature walk, even around your home.

1 hour = Take a nap.

half day = Take the afternoon off from work and do nothing productive.

1 day = Take a day trip to your favorite local attraction.

1 week = Plan a long vacation or staycation at home.

Competency

Moonshine, Mayberry, and Mechanics

"Never put a question mark where God puts a period."

—Richard Petty

SOMEWHERE BETWEEN THE FICTIONAL town of Mayberry and the ghosts of NASCAR past lies my childhood stomping grounds. Wilkes County, North Carolina has a fascinating history that intertwines moonshine, building cars to outrun the law, and the birth of NASCAR. It's also located thirty miles south of Mt. Airy, otherwise known as Mayberry on the classic *Andy Griffith Show*.

This current crisis has awakened my negative belief. "I'm not good enough, and I will fail." I didn't need a therapist to know where my insane level of workaholic, high responsibility, ADHD, anxiety, and so much neurosis came from. I'm a carbon copy of my dad—so much so that people used to stop me on the street and say, "I don't know your name, but I know who your dad is." There would be no need for a DNA test, but this wasn't a great compliment for a fifteen-year-old girl. While my dad definitely had genetic components of ADHD and anxiety, his fear of failure stemmed from being raised in an element of shame with no father in the early 1950s and in poverty. Even though I never missed a meal growing up, his fears were transferred to me. I've always had a huge fear of financial failure.

The roots for how we navigate through adverse times today are formed much earlier, deep in our history and biology. Most of our personality and coping mechanisms are hardwired by age eight. Now that's a sobering thought! How we make connections from birth to adulthood shapes us and builds resilience. This science is why I'm so passionate about my work with young children and their families. If we can set this up from the beginning, we can likely change the entire mental and physical health outcomes for generations of people.

My dad was a brilliant mechanic who crafted race car engines in the early years when NASCAR was in its infancy. If you've ever watched an episode of *The Andy Griffith Show* then you're familiar with Goober, the loveable, overly- friendly neighborhood mechanic. In several episodes, the people of Mayberry drive up to the filling station, blow the horn, rev the engine a few times, and then after a thoughtful second, Goober diagnoses the problem. Well, this scene was a frequent occurrence at my house, except the neighborhood mechanic was my dad.

Even though I have zero mechanical engineering abilities, and I still can't change my own tire (sorry, Dad, but thank you, AAA), I was completely fascinated by this entire process. I spent many a summer night hanging out in a steamy garage drinking a cold Grape Crush soda and watching my dad and his friends work on cars the way the cast of *Grey's Anatomy* works feverishly in surgery. Saturday nights were spent at a dirt racetrack with cotton balls stuffed in our ears to tolerate the deafening noise of revving engines, all while consuming french fries doused in ketchup and vinegar. The mecca of all these experiences was being allowed to go down to pit road where all the action went down. The precision, the teamwork, the split-second decision making, and the rush of exhilaration that came with victory was more energy than an elementary-school-age body could absorb. Some kids dreamed of backstage concert passes, but for a budding adrenaline junkie, this was it! I learned early on you can build the best race car, but your pit crew would ultimately win or lose the race for you. Every second counts.

As the years have evolved, we are living in a 24/7, drive-through, give-it-to-me-yesterday society. This pressure causes us to drive our bodies with the pedal to the metal as if there are no consequences, and we have no say over what impacts our bodies. Unlike our NASCAR counterparts, we only get one vehicle to travel in through life. How we treat our body and what happens to our body accumulates over time. Even the best-built machine needs pit stops along the way for new tires, gas, and even from time to time a swipe of the windshield to see where we're going. Unfortunately, most of our body vehicles only get an unscheduled pit stop when they break down from illness or the pressures of life.

Resilience Skill: Journal

What are you doing to take care of your physical health? Do you need to schedule a pit stop for a physical or begin some new healthy habits?

Replicating Emergency! for Mental Health

"Next to creating a life, the finest thing a man can do is save one."

—Abraham Lincoln

TODAY, YOU WILL CERTAINLY not find me in a garage teaching anyone how to build a race car engine, but you will find me in a classroom or on a stage teaching people how their bodies work. I've always had a love of health and how the human body works, and my dad passed on to me an insatiable need to find out what makes things tick. I still find a great many parallels between cars, racing, and our bodies. In hindsight, it's no wonder that I pursued a Master's in Public Health, but this was certainly not on the career wheel in my home economics classes. In the 1980s, if you loved studying health, your career choices were basically to become either a doctor or a nurse. No one could have predicted the explosion of science related to public health and prevention that would transform and save so many lives.

In the late 1970s while everyone was riding around North Carolina wearing no seatbelts and doctors were literally smoking in the rooms with patients, I was glued to the TV watching every single rerun of the hit show *Emergency!* I'm pretty sure this is the root of my love for all things triage medicine. Watching Desoto and Gage from Station 51 run calls and handle everything from snake bites to car crashes made my day. Every stuffed animal I ever owned has an extensive medical chart full of minor and complex injuries. The amount of Band Aids that my mother purchased over the years could likely have funded a few college textbooks.

It's hard to grasp now, but in 1972 when the show first aired, there really was no such thing as prehospital care for most Americans. Today, however, EMS is standard care for most areas of the US, but at that time, there were only twelve known paramedic units in all of North America. If someone needed to go to the hospital, you threw them in the car, whether they had a heart attack or massive bleeding, and just like on the racetrack, you floored it to the nearest hospital. In rural communities, this could mean up to a forty-five-minute or longer drive. This valuable time translates to lost heart tissues from cardiac arrest and lost brain tissue to strokes. Just like on the NASCAR pit road, every second counts, and valuable ones were lost in transport. This show was far more than entertaining—it inadvertently created a movement that continues to save lives today.

During my burnout with mental health work, I returned to school to complete my Master of Public Health. I went into this program in hopes of getting jobs to work with physical health issues such as heart disease, cancer, or diabetes … anything in which I didn't have to ask people about their emotions or feelings. Well, either I'm the unluckiest person around, or God has a wicked sense of humor, because this program wound up lighting a deeper fire in me for mental health work. This was my first exposure to research on Adverse Childhood Experiences, commonly referred to as ACEs. This research and biology literally hit me like a ton of bricks. Over the years, I had counseled case after case of women who worked two and three jobs and raised children, only to go on disability due to an autoimmune disorder or cancer. So many women I counseled for childhood sexual abuse also had complex medical issues. Now the science was connecting all the dots, and it was like watching all the lines in your paint by number life canvas being filled in.

ACEs are defined as stressful or traumatic events that children experience before age eighteen. Most often when we think of childhood trauma, we think of physical abuse, neglect, and sexual abuse. While these are certainly on the list, other childhood events are included. Some of these events labeled as ACEs may be surprising to many because they've become so commonplace in our society. such as divorce, living in poverty, parents with substance dependence, or a parent missing due to death or incarceration. All these add to the ACEs count, and they can cause long-term psychological and physiological damage. An ACE score is calculated by asking questions related to events that occurred prior to your eighteenth birthday. Each question is answered either YES or NO. For every YES response, you receive one point. At the end of the ten-question survey, your score is the total of all your responses. The goal here is a lot like golf, in that you want the lowest score possible.

For example, if someone had asked me five years ago if I had experienced trauma in my childhood, I would have said "No way. I had a picture-perfect childhood." However, as we look at the ACEs rating scale, growing up in a home with mental illness as I did is considered an ACE ... tick! Just like that, my scorecard begins to fill. While no adverse childhood experience is what we would hope for, the reality is that two out of three adults in the US have experienced one ACE. We've long suspected the psychological impacts of trauma leading to increased risk for mental illness and substance use disorders. However, recently the science is revealing concerning connections between childhood trauma and severe health consequences.

Growing bodies of research are demonstrating how traumatic events can literally change our brain and, in some cases, our very DNA. As the number of adverse childhood experiences goes up, so does the risk of not only mental illness and substance abuse but also heart disease, stroke, cancer, diabetes, and COPD. While I will never know for sure, I believe that my dad's colon cancer was the result of his high ACEs score.

Daily we're learning more about two amazing things: protective factors and the ability of the brain to heal from trauma. Protective factors are conditions in families and communities that serve as buffers, thereby increasing the health and well-being of children and families. These include social and emotional competence, social connections, concrete support, knowledge of parenting, and child development and resilience. So in comic book terms, ACEs are the villains, and protective factors are the superheroes! Great news for a child like me growing up with extensive mental illness in the family, these adverse experiences were offset by the presence of many of the protective factors above.

Equally encouraging is the almost daily research coming forth related to neuroplasticity, or the ability of the brain to heal from trauma. This is so helpful for people who have experienced trauma who might otherwise believe that the brain is hardwired and what happened to them can't be changed. Another wonderful development is that as therapists we're learning safer ways (called trauma-informed) to make treatment of traumatic events less stressful for people.

As we in the US are swimming upstream to battle an increasing opioid epidemic, here is a jaw-dropping statistic: having an ACE score of four or more increases the risk of injectable drug use greater than ten times those with no ACEs. You don't have to be a math whiz to interpret that this is an insane amount of risk. We can no longer see childhood trauma as just a sad and terrible social justice issue. It's at the root of many of our public health emergencies, such as addiction.

It's now commonplace that at any given event if someone goes into cardiac arrest, there are many people trained in CPR, and likely a defibrillator, nearby. We understand what it feels like to be faint and notice that our blood sugar or hydration may be off. So why do we know so little about our emotions and how to monitor our mental status? The brain is the largest organ in the body, with infinite capacity, yet we're given little guidance or education to assess and regulate this organ of the body. The pervasive belief is that emotional reactions are choices, and some are weak, and some are strong. Depressed people just need to try harder, and anxious people are wound too tight and just need to relax. We would never look at someone in cardiac arrest and go, "Hey, get it together, we all have chest pains from time to time."

I believe we have reached a point when the next wave of health education must be about our mental wellness. There's not a group of people who are crazy and another not crazy. That's a fallacy that continues to propagate the stigma and creates false senses of safety. Just like we all have a pulse, we all have mental status; if you're without a current mental status presentation, you're dead. The reality is that we all must manage our mental wellness, and if nothing else, the COVID pandemic has revealed that we are all vulnerable.

Thirty-five years later, both NASCAR and I have been through many changes, and I lost my favorite mechanic to cancer more than twenty years ago. What I wouldn't give for one more hot summer day infused with the smell of rubber, the sound of cars roaring around a track, and the look of pride on my dad's face as he shared his passion and history with his grandkids. My hope is that the science we have learned today regarding childhood trauma, along with a societal shift to preventative medicine, will allow many families more years to make memories.

Resilience Skills: Check your ACEs score.
www.acestoohigh.com

Digging Deep

"Upon my bed this is what I saw;
there was a tree at the center of the earth,
and its height was great. The tree grew great and strong,
its top reached to heaven, and it was visible to the ends of the
whole earth. Its foliage was beautiful, its fruit abundant,
and it provided food for all. The animals of the field found
shade under it, the birds of the air nested in its branches,
and from it all living beings were fed"

(Daniel 4:10–12)

IN NORTH CAROLINA, WE'RE known for our long leaf pine trees, which were of huge value to the shipbuilding industry in our early days. While I love biology, botany has never really given me a thrill, but how trees survive during droughts does fascinate me. To survive long droughts, pine trees rely on the established roots they already have to reach for deep water reserves in the ground.

I sit in my bed with my journal and colored pencils. I sketch out a tree complete with roots. I've done this art therapy activity with my clients many times over the years, but this is the first time I've done it for myself. As I sketch out my tree, I'm reminded of the forest of pine trees that surrounded my home growing up. A smile crosses my face as I recall many carefree days exploring those vast woods, when time meant nothing and the whole world was only what was before me in that moment.

It's a simple activity with no artistic talent needed. Simply draw a tree complete with branches and roots. Label the roots to represent people (living or gone) and experiences in your life that you can tap into to draw strength. Next, draw branches and label them with all the fruits of your life that these experiences have allowed you to achieve or become. Alongside the tree, draw people or things that support you now. In the sky, include things that would be needed for your self-care, such as rest, exercise, and time with friends to help nourish your tree. A huge part of resilience is drawing on past experiences to get you through present struggles. When we tap into former times when we were scared or overwhelmed, we find the courage to do it again. When we recall other days with high stress, we remember how we found calm.

I finish the last touches with colored pencils and feel a sense of peace. I now know why I use this tool so often with my clients—it gives me a sense of hope, something I haven't felt in weeks. When we're in crisis or depression, our brain can only focus on the negative, which blocks the ability of our mind to remember what we have survived and what we can do. I focus on my image and all the people and experiences that nourish and support my tree. I breathe in and out, and it's like a monsoon to my dry and weary spirit. My current wounded heart says, "I can't do it; I can't move forward." But my warrior past says, "Yes, yes, I can."

Dancing Dreams

A Dancer's Mind
The lights go down and the curtain rises,
My number is called and my heart skips a beat.
Will this be the performance of a lifetime,
Or will I once again suffer defeat?
My pulse races and inside I tremble,
But as the music begins, my body begins to feel
Every note, measure, and line
As my fate is soon to be sealed.
The judges look on intently
While the audience watches in awe,
But no matter how well the response,
It is still the judge's last call.
Many hours of dedication and practice
Have all come down to these
Three crucial minutes
To achieve my lifelong wish.
Many would say it is too great of a risk
And that the odds are simply too great:

Melissa Collins Harrell

But they have never had the desire
To challenge their own fate.
Step by step I make it through
One challenging minute at a time.
Soon I will finish and know
If the victory this time will be mine.
As the music ends and I strike a pose
And listen to the echo of cheers,
These are the beautiful sounds
That have encouraged me for years.
As I anxiously await the final decision,
I vow if I lose to never try again,
But deep in my heart I know
My main intent was never to win.

For I am a performer,
A dancer you see,
And that, for as long as I can remember,
Is all I have ever wanted to be.

—Melissa Collins Harrell, 1994

I WAS EIGHT YEARS old when my childhood friend Misty had her dance recital. I went along with our moms to watch her perform. I'd say that I can remember coming to the edge of my seat, but there really was no other choice. These were the kind of wooden auditorium seats that would flip back up on you, especially on an eight-year-old tiny body. As soon as the lights went up and the curtain opened, I was mesmerized, and I knew I absolutely had to do *that*. I must be a part of that. There was just something about the costumes, the movement, and the stage that called to me like a siren.

That fall I started ballet and tap classes. I was so excited each week to pack my clever dance bag. Some of you may have owned one of those perfect square boxes that housed your leotard, tights, and tap shoes in the tippy top, and the bottom had a special compartment just for your ballet slippers. You were a boss if you owned this bag. With both parents working and dance class being at four o'clock in the afternoon, the school bus would drop me off at my dance studio, and my parents would pick me up.

Big deal, you might say. Well, that was the first time I had ever ridden on a school bus not related to a field trip. I lived literally three doors down from my elementary school, and there was some bizarre rule that we weren't allowed to ride the school bus. I've never understood this policy, as if it would take extra gas to pick me up, but it was a real thing. One of my parents would drop us off at school and then we would walk home. Thankfully, it wasn't both ways uphill or in the snow, but it had some pretty good perks. To get to my house, I had to walk by Aunt Betty's house as well as Granny's house. As you can imagine, a girl can work up quite a thirst walking home, so I needed to stop in and get some water at each location, which generally also included a piece of cake or a cookie, because of course I looked so hungry and pitiful. Note, dancers have a few acting skills in their bags.

Not only did I board the bus and get off at the dance studio, but I dressed myself and put my hair in a ponytail at age eight. We certainly didn't' have cell phones, and my parents didn't call the studio to see if I arrived safely. GASP! Note also that The Hutchins School of Dance was located across the street from John Boy's BBQ, where I crossed the street alone to get a snack on several occasions.

Taking dance classes was the best part of my week. There was nothing better than dance day. It would be many years later before I'd learn the neuroscience behind movement and mental wellbeing. I had no idea that as my carefree body twirled and moved for what I deemed to be fun, my brain was processing my day, my week, and resetting me in ways that would serve me positively. When we participate in physical activity, it increases the feel-good chemicals of our brain. Movement is our natural antidepressant and can have a significant impact on mild to moderate depression and anxiety.

Ballet, while beautiful to watch, is one of the most sadistic things a human can do to their body. It's literally unnatural to teach your body to execute everything from a turned out versus parallel position. And have you ever looked at the feet of a ballerina? They're hideous; it's like a train wreck. Don't look!

One of the defining moments of a ballerina's life, whether you dance for a few years or become a professional, is the day you get your first pair of pointe shoes, or as they're often called in the South, "your toe shoes." Each year in the spring, my teacher would call a few girls into her office, and you knew that this was the moment you'd get to go en pointe. The thrill of getting a driver's license didn't hold a candle to this day.

The excitement soon gives way to struggle, complete with blisters and your pretty pink satin shoes stained with blood. You learn very early on that you don't baby these injuries. Nope, no ointment, no Band Aids. You let that skin get used to the friction of the shoes creating thicker skin. This parallels so well with resilience. We know that there will be struggles, just like a dancer knows, but we can't hide them or shield ourselves from it all. My therapist once told me that she wouldn't be surprised to find out that I practiced self-flagellation, which is a religious practice of inflicting physical pain as spiritual discipline. To which I responded, "Oh yes, I did … it's called ballet!"

My love for ballet was a double-edge sword in my life. It would build in me discipline and an incredible work ethic; however, it also reinforced my core belief that I needed to be perfect. Ballet demands nothing less than perfection. There is no such critique as "That was good enough." You run the same variation over and over, and once you nail the perfect double pirouette, the quest begins for the triple, and so it continues on and on in a never-ending cycle of achievement.

A classical ballet class always follows a specific order. The combinations may change, but the order remains the same, which for a Type A anxious person brings a lot of comfort. Class begins at the barre to prepare your body for the work to come. Next you transition to the center of the room for stretches and combinations, followed up with turns and great leaps across the floor, and finally rounded out by a beautiful ritual of reverence to the teacher and accompanist. The very act of stepping to the ballet barre, feet in second position, hand touching barre, and music beginning instantly grounded me. There were no racing thoughts of pressing school assignments, no thoughts of what boy would call or what was going on at home. To this day it still works; the worries and stressors may have changed, but the muscle memory still works like a charm.

I reflect on my childhood experiences often as I look at our efforts to build resiliency skills in children today. Even as independent as I have tried to raise my children, I'm not sure that I would have believed it was OK for an eight-year-old to dress herself, get on a bus, and be dropped off at a dance studio. But I did it, and I don't remember being scared to ride on the bus. I'm sure it was a little intimidating at first, but all I knew was that I had to get to that dance studio, and if it meant boarding that bus, fear was conquered. I never thought that I "could" or "couldn't" do that, and by their choice, my parents allowed me to do this, which enforced in my brain that this was OK. These are the things that build confidence and resilience—little steps that say, "You can do this without assistance." I would tap into this memory of a brave eight-year-old girl years later when I stepped on a plane to fly halfway around the world to do something that, just like dancing, I couldn't explain, but I just knew deep in my soul I had to do it.

Resilience Skill: Grounding

One of the quickest ways to calm the mind and get into the present is called grounding. A very popular and easy one to remember is called the 5-4-3-2-1 Grounding Technique.

5: Look: Look around your immediate surroundings and name five things you see out loud.

4: Feel: Notice and name aloud four feelings or sensations related to your body. *My hands feel cold. I feel the back of the chair touching my back.*

3: Listen: Listen for three sounds and say them aloud.

2: Smell: Name two things you smell. If there's nothing, think of two favorite scents and say them aloud.

1: Taste: Say one thing aloud that you can taste; if nothing, say your favorite thing to taste.

You're Going to Major in What?

I WAS JUST AS surprised as anyone else that I decided to major in dance, possibly more surprised. As much as I loved dancing, I never dreamed of being a professional dancer. While others apparently saw this graceful swan that was born to dance, the reflection I saw in the mirror felt more like the ugly duckling.

Secretly, deep down I never felt that I had the raw talent it would take. Like in most areas, I was an overachiever, worked hard, and was a fake-it-til-you-make-it kind of girl. Not to mention that I'm a small-town girl who ... gasp ... never wanted to live in New York or Los Angeles, so that would leave me out of the big leagues in the dance world.

My first love was medicine. I've already confessed my obsession for the show *Emergency!* I also consumed large volumes of *Marcus Welby* and slept each night in personalized PJs that replicated scrubs from the hit show *MASH*, which revolved around a US Mobile Army Surgical Hospital (MASH) in the Korean War. I mean, really, couldn't I just watch *Bugs Bunny*? In middle school, on a dot matrix printer, I made a sign that I proudly hung on my door that read: "*Quiet, future pediatrician at work.*" My entire high school career was dedicated to getting into college with the goal of medical school. Not one passing thought of dancing for the NYC ballet or on Broadway.

In eighth grade we created a career goal folder, and I wrote an essay. This was the 1980s version of a vision board.

Here's what I wrote:

Who I Want To Be

After I graduate from high school, I want to attend Surry Community College. After two years here I want to transfer to Wake Forest University and attend Bowman Gray School of Medicine. Next, I would like to go two more years to complete my education as a pediatrician. During this education period, I would like to win some scholarship money by being in pageants.

After school I would like to get married and have one or two children. I would like to live in a nice home and have a cocker spaniel puppy.

My tenth-grade year was hyper-focused on two things: getting selected for the summer Governor's School Experience and getting accepted to the NC School of Science and Math. In North Carolina, Governor's School is a state-sponsored summer program for gifted students from across the state to have a six-week mini college experience. I auditioned to study dance as my main area, but we also spent time in philosophy and current events symposiums. The NC School of Science and Math is a free state-sponsored high school that offers more challenging coursework for high school juniors and seniors. In the 1980s, there were no online classes or early college experiences for high school students beyond a few AP courses. Even though I would have to move over two hours away from home to attend, for me, being from a rural area with limited resources, this would increase my chances of later getting into medical school. If I could get in and do well there, I might not only get into a great college but also get scholarships.

So the pressure was real. Not only did I strive for all As but the highest average possible. Well, this great pursuit landed me exactly where I wanted to go eventually on my dream sheet: The Bowman Gray School of Medicine at Wake Forest University ... but not as a student. As a patient. All the pressure to juggle so many balls and maintain perfection had created excruciating stomach pain, which was rapidly diagnosed as stomach ulcers. The pediatrician we worked with began to berate my parents for putting so much pressure on a young child, but I quickly intervened to let her know that this pressure was all me. My parents were always supportive of my academic pursuits, but these were intrinsic pressures that had nothing to do with them. No, I took full responsibility.

Finally I was referred for counseling, learned coping skills, and put this runaway train to a screeching halt. Survey says ... WRONG! This was 1988, and psychological care for anyone was far from routine practice. Not only was my obvious Generalized Anxiety Disorder (GAD) left untreated, but no one ever educated me or my parents in either the medical or education community on the special emotional impacts that come with giftedness. Children who are gifted often struggle with overexcitability, emotional intensity, and perfectionism. These qualities can also lead to social frustrations or boredom, as it's difficult to connect to age-appropriate topics that peers want to discuss. Perfectionism is the root of the anxiety, and it starts young. Well-meaning teachers and parents praise you for "being smart," and then your whole identity becomes that concept. Who will you be if you are less than perfectly smart?

It has taken me years to unravel the web of all these qualities and how they impact my life and relationships. To have known this information as a high school or even college student could have saved me countless doctor's visits for stress induced ailments such as ulcers, migraines, and IBS. Possibly I wouldn't have been sick in bed every year and winter and spring break after running myself completely into the ground. I also could have given myself more permission and grace to enjoy simple things. I'm certain that this will resonate with many of my readers.

I also wonder if I'd been referred during that time if I would have been misdiagnosed as having ADHD or possibly a mood disorder, particularly given my family history. After all, I've questioned this about myself many times over the years. Even now, knowing more, I always tell audiences to bear with me because my ADHD will shine through. With no clear diagnosis, and no coping skills to address my issues, my cycles of overachieving would continue unchecked for years. I should have come with a warning label that read "Danger Ahead" because the runaway train was on the loose again with the threat of derailment around every corner.

Resilience Skill: Monitoring

Keep a monitor on your mental wellbeing, just like your blood pressure. Use a simple rating scale of 1–10. Ask yourself how anxious/depressed/angry/stressed you are each day on your scale. Awareness is the first key to better management.

Finding My Way

"All that is gold does not glitter;
Not all who wander are lost.
The old that is strong does not wither.
Deep roots are not reached by the frost."

—J.R.R. Tolkien, *The Fellowship of the Ring*

I WAS ACCEPTED INTO both NC Governor's School and NC School of Science and Math. I absolutely adored Governor's School. If I had to choose a time experience in my life to be frozen in, like in *The Twilight Zone*, that's probably where I'd choose. For an artist and gifted brain, it was a bit like being in your own Greco Roman environment. I was able to dance every day, create choreography, and travel across the state performing. For this moment in time, we were professionals. We rolled out dance floors in all kinds of places, like giving a sunset performance on the beach. Like I said, living the dream. As an adult, it still sounds like bliss—having no bills or responsibilities other than performing and debating philosophy.

It was also an incredible time of social and emotional explosion. I had never lived or met people outside of Wilkes County.

To learn about where others lived and to encounter new ideas and beliefs was refreshing but also shocking and intimidating.

I wound up having two roommates, as we had a corner room. My first roommate, Valerie walked in wearing a red slip. Yes, I kid you not, a red slip like you wore under your dress back in the day. It was shocking enough that she didn't have a dress on over her slip, but perish the thought, I didn't know they made slips in any color other than beige or white. And she had bright red lipstick to boot. Surely she wasn't from the South, or her mama didn't get the memo.

She started unpacking her things, and my eyes were getting larger by the minute. I kept running down the hall to find my friend Laura, from my high school, to update her on the various items she was unpacking. I informed Laura that clearly my new roommate was Wiccan because she was placing statues of witches all around the room. I was in a panic. What was I going to do? I mean, I was Southern Baptist—we do not do witches. What if I was about to become a part of a cult sacrifice?

As it turned out, Valerie was not Wiccan, and I wasn't sacrificed on the night of the full moon. However, Valerie's resume did include being a witch—that is, the Wicked Witch in the *Wizard of Oz*. She was there as a theater concentration. She had just completed a run in her role and had a lot of memorabilia to show.

I had less than two weeks between returning from Gov School and moving into NCSSM. Initially I loved NCSSM. While it was a hard transition to move away at sixteen, I loved the challenges. But as time went on, I missed dancing so much. They had just built a beautiful dance studio there, but no classes, and I wasn't allowed off campus at the times of day that classes were offered for my level. To cope with the intense pressures, I would spend hours dancing in the studio. My classmates would often come to peer through the two-way window to watch my informal private sessions. One day a girl asked me why I wasn't at the NC School of the Arts. My answer was because I wanted to go into medicine, and this was just my hobby. I remembered walking away, toe shoes slung over my shoulder, thinking how crazy I would be to get a degree in dance. What would I do with that?

As the months pressed on, the days grew longer and more difficult. I began to have a difficult time focusing, and I felt like I just couldn't keep up with all the mounting assignments. Meanwhile back home, my mom was spiraling deeper into her own dark well of clinical depression. She was struggling to work, and this was the beginning of her eventual disability due to her mental health. There was also a lot of tension between my parents, and I was disconnected from my sister as well.

No one had cell phones back in the day. We had one payphone in our dormitory hall, and we had to take turns calling. Calls home were long distance, and we used prepaid calling cards to pay for our calls. There was absolutely no privacy; everyone heard your entire life. It didn't help that every time I got on the phone, my mom would start to cry because of her depression and she missed me. I would shut down my feelings and felt horrible that I couldn't be there to support her. Never realizing that I was missing the parent to support me, evermore the hyper responsible child as parent and fixer of all.

The Power of Words

"I have learned that people will forget what you said, people will forget what you did, but people will never forget how you made them feel."

—Maya Angelou

THIS QUOTE HANGS IN my office to remind me every day of the power of words.

In February of my junior year of high school, I made one of the most grueling decisions of my life. I left NCSSM and returned home. It was a proverbial catch- 22. I wasn't happy there, yet I wasn't sure that I belonged back home in my old environment. I felt so incredibly lost and like a huge failure. In reflection now, I know that I was sinking into serious clinical depression and really needed some mental health support. But it was 1989, and that just wasn't talked about. If it was, people with depression were weak. Remember, I still had no idea of all the emotional liabilities that came with giftedness, even at a school like NCSSM, a school full of these types of kids. No one talked or counseled with us regarding these issues, not to mention my ever-increasing family stressors.

Once I arrived home, the spiral into depression continued. In the midst of what would be normal teenage angst already, I had lost what little identity I had and was in a pit of despair. My whole life plan was blown up, and I didn't know what to do to get it back on course. In the proverbial all or nothing, my life was over before it started. Not to mention my home life was completely depressing. I did everything I could to not be home.

I had mixed feelings about returning to East Wilkes, my former high school. To the best of my memory, I don't remember telling anyone to jump off a bridge or "So long, suckers" before I left. I just knew I wouldn't have the selection of classes and opportunities I had just left. Again, I didn't know where I belonged. I wasn't just a fish out of water—I was like a polar bear trying to live in South Florida.

I remember sitting in history class one of my first days back when suddenly Brent Hincher walked over and slid into the seat in front of me. He turned around with his sparkly eyes and said, "Hey, how's it going?" This act in and of itself was no big deal, as I had known Brent my whole life. He was the kid who would tug your pigtails but then flash you that smile he hoped would innocently convey that he was just playing. Being classmates since kindergarten in a small rural community, we had that long-term school bond where you know who ate the paste in first grade and who made out with who at the eighth-grade dance.

I really don't remember my response to him, but I will never forget his. He said that he was glad I was back and that I was missed. This was such a revelation; I had never thought that I'd been missed by anyone at my former high school. I just assumed that I was gone without a trace, as if I'd never existed there. True to Maya Angelou's words, you never forget that feeling of being validated and affirmed. It was a pivotal moment for me and helped me shift from existing to assimilating back into my old high school culture. Instead of starting anew, I felt permission to return to my rightful place in my class. Finally, I belonged somewhere.

I started to reconnect with old friends as well as build new friendships. The summer before my senior year, I got a job at a local grocery store. Yes, of course, the high end one that was Granny approved. I didn't try out for cheerleading; instead, I played tennis. Not only was I not good at it, but I was horrible! My coach was constantly telling me to get off my toes. It was like watching a bad version of *Swan Lake* run around swatting a racquet at flies. I didn't care; it was fun. Wow, I don't have to be good at everything. I don't have to succeed. People like me for who I am, not what I can achieve. As a matter of fact, I think they liked me better.

I began to let my guard down and not worry so much and just be a teenager. I started hanging out more socially and flirting with the ideas that parents worry teens will do. I was smitten by my James Dean boyfriend and living my best teenage life, breaking all the rules I never thought I would.

It was during that time that I first discovered what I thought were the benefits of alcohol. While it's as old as time for young people to experiment with alcohol, for someone who is extremely driven and highly anxious, experimentation can be the beginning of a lifelong struggle. You take that first drink and suddenly that feeling subsides—no pressure, no racing thoughts, and whew, I can relax. I spend a lot of time educating people that you can either use the right clinically sound anxiety meds or people will find their own. People are going to find some way to cope with anxiety, depression, or pain.

Somehow despite my rebellious ways, I still managed to graduate in the top ten of my class and was accepted to a few colleges. By this time, my mom was basically checked out due to her mental illness, so for financial reasons I decided it would be best to attend the local community college. I taught dance for my dance teachers and decided to set my sights on nursing school. Given the financial situation, the long years to achieve medical school just seemed like a lost dream. Not only did I want to be a nurse, but my goal was to be a flight nurse. Yep, you guessed it, once again put me right where all the trauma is happening.

I applied to the same RN school that my mom had attended just a few years earlier. When I walked into my interview, I recognized Mrs. King not only as Mom's former nursing instructor but also as a parent of one of my current dance students. Again, welcome to rural NC. We exchanged pleasantries about how my mom was doing and how well her daughter recently did in our annual dance recital. Once we started the formal interview, there were the typical questions of why I wanted to be a nurse and did I understand the demand of this type of program. In my head I answered, "Lady, have you seen my transcript? I love torture; sign me up." But my response was more like, "I absolutely want to be in this program."

As I listened to the acceptance steps for the program, her next response really took me by surprise. At our recent dance recital, I had performed several solo routines as time fillers for younger students to change, and she was apparently very impressed with my artistic talents. She asked me if I'd ever considered a career in dance. Wait, what? A career? In dance? Weren't we here to talk about nursing school? You know, IVs, meds, and bedpans, not tutus and tap shoes.

There was a small window of time before I had to claim my spot in the nursing program, and she encouraged me to take that time to ask myself if I was really done with dance. She said, "You have your whole life ahead of you to become a nurse but only a small window to pursue a dance career."

She had planted more than one seed. I had never thought that dance could be anything more than a hobby. You can imagine after all this intense pursuit and preparation for a medical career, the reaction from my dad after two years of college when I announced that I'd like to change my major from pre-med to dance. I'm pretty sure that date is etched on a calendar with the full Richter scale value in Western NC. After a deep lecture of life instruction on how difficult it is to live out of a cardboard box under a bridge, my dad stormed out to work in the garden or tinker on a car and do anything but deal with me.

Before you write my dad off as this cruel parent, remember his negative cognitions. He grew up with a single mom in poverty, and he had worked very hard, often two jobs, to afford us better opportunities. He feared those financial struggles for his daughter, but hey, I was twenty with this whole new world that had opened up to me. Scary but exciting at the same time. After he left, I turned and braced for round two from my mom. It wasn't what I expected at all. She told me I had my whole life to do many things and that I should have a job in something that brought me joy. On a side note of wisdom she said, "but only if you major in dance education." The education degree eventually opened the door to counseling. Mama does know best!

The Crowning Moment

"If you give up on your dreams, what's left?"

—Jim Carrey

BY 1993, I HAD completed one portion of that eight-grade vision board, which was to attend Surry Community College. However, the rest of the plan had taken more than a slight detour. It was the summer before I was to transfer to my dream school of Wake Forest University, which was now East Carolina University. ECU is a state university located in Greenville, NC. It originally started as a teacher's training college but now offers a vast array of degrees and conducts cutting edge research. I was sold on attending ECU the moment I stepped on campus. It was a large university with a small college feel, and luckily for me it had a strong dance program.

That summer as I prepared to move, I was cast as the lead dancer in *My Fair Lady* back in Mount Airy. This was such a blessing for many reasons, but the main one was that it kept me out of my house. A black cloud hovered over my house. My mom's depression was deepening, and being in my house was beyond gloom and doom. Even now writing this I feel my heart rate increase and heaviness in my chest as I think about it. I never knew what version of my mom I would get when I walked in the door. She could be crying or bite your head off for asking her how she was doing; everything I said was the wrong thing. Watching her struggle to get up and get dressed, listening to the constant arguing between my parents over her not working and money, was just too much.

Anyone who has participated in theater life knows that your cast becomes your second family, as you spend a lot of time together. This cast became my surrogate family and shelter. We all need connection. Youth groups, sports, and the arts are great connections for youth. This same need for connection is also what draws kids to gangs. The theater was a place I felt understood and I belonged. Long nights of rehearsal allow for connections and inside jokes that only the cast knows.

Another given in theater is that a diva will emerge in every cast. Our diva, as we shall call her, was named Summer. She began to talk about doing the Miss Mount Airy pageant, which was a preliminary to the Miss NC pageant. Mount Airy is the home of Andy Griffith and the model for the town of Mayberry. So, in essence, the winner of the Miss Mount Airy title was Miss Mayberry. Even though that had previously been on my dream sheet, I had closed out my quest for Miss America a while back. The year before I had participated in the same pageant, and as my teenagers say, it was an epic fail. Most of these girls had been doing this since birth. I was so happy to leave that stage, put my jeans on, and get a burger with my friends. I said I never wanted to do that again.

As Summer began to tell everyone that she was going to do the pageant and she had it in the bag, the peer pressure began. "You must do it! Please, she needs some competition." Eventually I caved and decided to give it one more try. My desire to compete was met with indifference from my parents. If it didn't cost them any money, they didn't care. Plus, my dad was still reeling from my decision to change from premed to dance. "Please, don't even talk about pageants." I went to the bank and withdrew the last few hundred dollars I had left in my account. I rented a bright orange evening gown that had been worn on the Miss America stage and wore an old dance costume in my closet to a self-choreographed tap number to "Stuff Like That There" by Bette Midler.

My goal was to win first runner up, take the scholarship money, and never look back. So long! As the competition came to the final awards, I became keenly aware that I might win. Once the first runner up was announced and it wasn't me, I was like, "Oh my, this is about to happen." When that crown went on my head, it was the most intoxicating feeling, but not why most people would think. For me it was like "Wow, something looked like what I thought on my dream sheet." I had forgotten how good it felt to set a goal and achieve it. After years of licking her wounds, the cheetah had made a kill again, and she felt alive.

My walk down the runway was nearly shattered in second grade by a broken nose. True story—running back to line after a tornado drill. I loved bumping into my second grade teacher right after the Miss NC pageant that year and her saying that when she saw me on TV she thought, "I'm sure glad we got that nose fixed." You got to love a caring teacher. Unfortunately, the rush of this win didn't last long. My mom walked up on stage and the photographer set us up for a mother/daughter photo. She put her arm around my waist and leaned in and whispered in my ear, "How could you do this to me?" Within seconds the thrill of exhilaration and joy was replaced with an old but familiar childhood feeling of shame and guilt, as if I'd done something wrong. I turned to look at her in disbelief right as the photographer snapped the photo.

Gleaning the Good

"Your big opportunity may be right where you are now."

—Napoleon Hill

THERE ARE A LOT of opinions and negative images surrounding pageants. Shows like *Toddlers and Tiaras* and *Dance Moms* certainly haven't helped. I'm not here to debate those issues or deny that others had very harsh experiences. I can only speak about my personal journey. Just like any other sport or competitive endeavor, there are situations of abuse and personal strife. However, there are many women out there like me who are better for having participated in certain systems. For me, participating in the Miss America System in the early 1990s was a huge part of my story

In the early 1990s, the Miss America Organization made a radical shift from traditional pageantry. The image of Miss America pivoted from Barbie Doll in a beaded sequin gown to a sharp dressed businesswoman in a public relations position. At this time, we rarely wore our crowns at public events. We dressed in business suits and were very active in community service in our represented areas. My first community services platform was with Habitat for Humanity, and my second platform was "Character

Counts," for which I was awarded a community service award for at the state level.

Holding a local title was also a full-time job. I learned to balance my full college load and working full-time. There were speaking engagements, community events, and preparation for Miss NC, which helped me to grow my window of tolerance during this time. I attribute my ability to handle a full load with grace under pressure to this intense season of growth. I learned to work out and take care of myself. I learned how to market myself and the business skills that I would have never learned in school, like how to speak on a dime and feel comfortable in almost any situation. Job interviews aren't anxiety provoking after you've been drilled by a CNN firing squad on every issue known to humanity.

I couldn't have asked for a better committee than my Mount Airy family. This committee was my family during a very crucial time in my life. They were there to support me while my mom's depression led to her hospitalization. The night I won, her reason for saying that awful comment to me was that she had put our family in debt again with her bipolar spending. She knew we didn't have the finances to purchase the things I would need for Miss NC. My dad had already busted his butt to pay off her spending one time, and now she'd be forced to tell him again. I was told by my committee to focus on my classes at ECU and prepare for competition; meanwhile, they raised all the funds to buy beyond what I needed for Miss NC.

After competing at Miss NC, I really thought that would be it. I came, I saw, I conquered … time to move on to the next adventure. It wasn't long until I decided to try one more time for that shot to walk the Miss America stage. I didn't want to sit back one day in my rocking chair and wonder what if I'd tried just one more time. Talk about resilience training … this victory didn't come easily. I did five preliminary competitions, placing first runner up in three and finally winning the fifth. I'm not ashamed to say that my exhausted body slept with that crown by my bed like an Olympic gold medal!

As Miss Duplin County, I had another incredible committee of volunteers. With my "Character Counts" community service program, I was in a public school several times a week and spent hundreds of hours running educational classes on good citizenship traits and supported the drug resistance training program, DARE. Funny how God just works things right out in what seems like the most unlikely places. Who would have thought that a pageant tiara would lead me to my lifelong calling? This experience gave me the opportunity to work with some of the finest school counselors I've ever known. They opened their hearts and shared their wisdom with me regarding how to support the social and emotional development of children in schools. Their passion for children led me to fall in love with counseling and confirmed a flicker in me that had been noticed a few years earlier.

While doing my student teaching in a rural middle school, my mentor teacher sat down with me one day and talked about how I seemed drawn to the social and emotional needs of the kids. She inquired if I'd ever considered school counseling and encouraged me to consider a graduate program. I'd never even thought of getting an advanced degree, especially in counseling. I will always be grateful to Gina for noticing this and kindling that initial fire. When you see potential in people, let them know. You never know where that might lead,

I never wore a state or national crown, but I did win the first Miss America Educational Scholarship for those seeking graduate degrees to work in education. There will never be a price on what this program offered to me. I didn't need to walk away with another crown to embrace an arsenal of business skills and the ability to market myself. With my scholarship money I embarked on my next challenge—graduate school for, you guessed it, counseling.

The Making of a Therapist

"The nature of humanity, its essence is to feel another's pain as one's own, and to act to take that pain away. There is nobility in compassion, a beauty in empathy, a grace in forgiveness."

—John Connolly

WHILE I'M CONTINUALLY HUMBLED that God would use my life this way, this was most assuredly not where I saw myself landing. For me, counseling is this sacred place where God drew all my crazy passions that seemed to have no connection at all into a gift. Being a therapist has brought me a deep sense of purpose in my life, but it has also left me vulnerable to other people's pain. I tell people all the time that graduate school isn't about the most intelligent people—it's about perseverance. It's literally a marathon event. Possibly the original reality show, *Survivor*, was based on graduate school.

I literally danced my way through grad school by working in a local preschool and ballet school. My mornings were full of thirty-minute classes of energy-filled preschoolers, and the evenings with intense classes in classical ballet, tap, and jazz. I often refer to this as a very sweet season of my life. While full of activity, there were so many wonderful experiences. I was very fortunate to be teaching in a true classical ballet school that still produced two full-length ballets a year, including *The Nutcracker*. It had always been my dream to dance in *The Nutcracker* ballet, but the opportunity never arose. Not only did I get to dance in this beloved ballet, but I also became the assistant artistic director and choreographer for five years. It was such a blessing because my director, who was a huge supporter of education and had a Master's herself, would allow me each semester to arrange my dance classes around my grad courses.

In the summer, I'd teach half-day dance camps and then make the one-hour commute to Campbell University in Buies Creek, NC. Perish the thought, there were no online classes—you had to actually physically show up and sit in your seat week after week. On a sweltering July day, likely with one minute to spare before class began, I slid into the seat of my counseling class. My professor announced that we were going to do role plays. As she scanned the room for volunteers, I waved my hand, like I was hailing a taxi in NYC: "Oh, please pick me." It should be noted that all the energy I had that day had been sucked out by preschoolers in tutus at dance camp, so I had just consumed a large Mountain Dew and Snickers bar on my way to this 6:00–10:00 night class. The caffeine and sugar rush were at optimal blood level for excessive volunteerism.

My classmate Michael took his scenario and read it. We placed our chairs back-to-back to simulate a crisis hotline.

Professor: *Ring ... ring!*

Me: Crisis line. This is Melissa. To whom am I speaking?

Michael: Michael.

Me: Hello, Michael, I'm so glad you called tonight. This is a totally confidential call. How may I help you?

Michael: I was walking back to my dorm and this guy grabbed me out of nowhere and …

A long pause

Me: Michael, are you still there?

Michael: Yes.

Me: It's OK … please continue.

Michael: It's just so embarrassing.

Me: Take your time. Michael, where are you now?

Michael: In my room.

Me: Are you safe?

Michael: Yes (he begins to cry). He raped me … the mother $&))7* raped me.

Me: Michael … stay on the line. I'm going to stay right here.

At that moment, all my classmates faded away, and, in my mind there was no one in the room but me and Michael. Mountain Dew had nothing on this high. I had so easily tapped into this familiar thread; the trauma junkie was awakened.

Like most professions, you don't learn how to do therapy in school. Sure, we learn theories and models and do role plays, but your clients teach you how to be a therapist. I once had a relative tell me that it must be nice to get paid to just talk to people all day instead of doing hard work. "Yeah, Rob, it's a really good deal. You should check into it." I like to think of a therapy session as a verbal tennis match. The goal is to keep the conversation going with very few net balls. Remember, I did have that one glowing season in high school!

After graduate school, my first paid job was in an elementary school. I loved being a school counselor, but boy could I have used some lessons on boundaries and compassion fatigue. Remember the runaway train? Yep, still speeding ahead to danger. I'd do all the things to assist my students all day and take home paperwork at night. I was beyond burning the candle at both ends. As fully documented here, this wasn't my first wake up call to how stress and burnout can impact your body, but it was the most serious to date.

One Thursday night after a full day at the elementary school and then seeing clients in private practice till around 9:00 p.m., I came home to unwind. After days full of hearing other people's problems and guiding them to solutions, it's very hard to turn your brain off. My dinner consisted of a bowl of popcorn and a glass of wine. I enjoyed my weekly episode of *ER* and basked in the joy that the next day was Friday. A few hours later, I woke up and was literally the star of my own episode of *ER*. I remembered getting up and going to the bathroom and then trying to make my way back to the bed … and then nothing. The next time I woke up I was being wheeled into the back of an ambulance with full IVs in motion. My brain was processing and thinking, "Uh oh, this is probably not good."

In my craziness of the day before, I hadn't eaten and didn't even realized that I had barely had anything to drink. For future reference, popcorn and wine will not offset these issues. I had experienced a major syncope episode, a fancy medical term for passing out, due to severe dehydration. I paid a ridiculously high deductible to be told what my mama taught since childhood: drink plenty of water.

For a while I took it very seriously and was much better about taking care of myself. Then I moved from the school full-time to working full-time in private practice. This pace of life is so different, and sadly the very nature of this business sets you up to not take care of yourself. As a friend of mine used to say, "You eat what you kill." When you're only getting paid if you're in front of a client, you're going to do what it takes to see people. With the craziness of battling with health insurance companies and people not showing for appointments, you pack your days with back-to-back clients to make it all work. Rarely did anyone take lunch. I used to keep a jar of peanut butter in the kitchen and eat it straight from the jar in between clients.

Even with the insanity, I loved private practice. Every client was a new puzzle to solve. During my first year, I was pregnant with my first child, so I would see clients in the evenings and spend the next day before work reading and studying up on treatment models. This was a great rhythm and easy to juggle because my kid was in utero and therefore not too demanding. Then life got interesting. It was baby one, then two, and finally three. The flexibility I had to be home with the kids was great, but it also made for some very long days. By day I was a mother basically running her own home daycare until the babysitter came around 3:30. Then I'd head to my office and start seeing clients at 4:00 and end at 9:00 or 10:00 at night. *Clickety clack*, the stress train is racing down the track.

Resilience Skill: Back to the Basics

HOW ARE YOU DOING EATING/ HYDRATING/ SLEEPING/MOVING?

Finding My Mind

"Lose your mind and come to your senses."

—Fritz Perls

JUGGLING A FULL-TIME CAREER, three kids, a partner, home, and volunteer activities are enough to drive any woman to insanity. Couple that with those insane ideals of perfectionism, intensity, and traumas that were still untreated from my childhood, and we have a real show for you ladies and gentlemen.

I'm not a huge comic book fan, but I live in a house full of them. By way of osmosis, I've acquired more knowledge than I could ever hope for related to these characters. I know that Batman chose to become his own most feared creature, the bat, because as a child he fell into a cave and was attacked by bats. I guess if I were to become a comic book character she would have to be called "Stress Woman" because this is the nemesis I've battled my whole life.

Each day I would get up to do this "Working Mom Life" and glance in the mirror. The reflection was far from the Wonder Woman superhero of my childhood. In her place I saw a tattered Stress Woman cape, bags under my eyes, and certainly no chiseled physique. Who has time to work out? Running late was as close as I got to a real exercise routine these days. It wasn't that I thought everyone around me had it all together, because I was fortunate enough to have real mom friends and we just spoke the truth. But deep down, I craved stillness and peace even for just a moment. I was always striving and struggling to find that balance between being present with my family, giving to my job, and doing the things I really wanted to do for me. Not to mention the outside demands already discussed about dealing with my mentally ill family, who lived two hundred miles across the state. Not going to lie … the distance helped at times.

Just as we try different diet and exercise plans, I've spent most of my adult life attempting to slow down, better manage my stress, and repeating this cycle a few hundred times. Let the irony not be lost that my job was and continues to be to help people do this every single day. I defend myself with the proverbial quote, "Physician, heal thyself." My success and failures are of course documented in a few hundred journals. I've tried not to sweat the small stuff, observed a Sabbath, and even the Hebrew day planner, which totally didn't work because I still struggle to understand daylight savings time!

In the early 2000s as I was training to become a therapist, we viewed stress and taught stress management differently. The past methods we used encouraged people to cut down on their amount of stress. While this is effective, it's really only one small piece because we simply can't get rid of some of our stressors. If you have a health condition, children, family caregiving duties, financial obligations, or car troubles, it would be nice to just cross them off the list, but that's not reality. The more we learn regarding brain science, the more we understand that stress itself isn't the biggest problem but rather the way we respond to the stress in our life has drastic impacts on our mental and physical health.

Earlier in Biology 101 Basics, we reviewed the "Fight or Flight" function of our body. This was designed to keep us safe and gets triggered whenever we feel threatened. This triggered response releases an army of hormones, including adrenaline, epinephrine, and cortisol. This response is perfect if you're about to fight a tiger but not as useful when your computer decides to do twenty updates and your boss wanted a report two hours ago, or your toddler throws down on aisle five with everyone staring, or you just got rejected for a promotion you were counting on.

Our bodies were designed only to run this "Flight or Fight" mode in emergencies, but the stress we live under today keeps our bodies running on this emergency setting more frequently than they should. It's like propping your car on blocks and setting a brick on the accelerator of a car and leaving it running wide open. The parts to this car will wear out way quicker and suffer more damage than with proper use and maintenance of the car.

The marketing in our society is crafty and leads us to believe that the way to relieve stress is to step away from our lives. We get sucked into binge watching Netflix, going to entertaining events, shopping, or scrolling for hours on our phones. Not that in moderation these things are bad, but they are just distractions. They don't address the chemicals and tensions in our body that are pent up from accumulated stress. If not released, these are the things that create pain and disease. Stress is at the root of many of our current health issues. Fatigue, burnout, anxiety, addiction, and chronic illness can all be linked to stress. While the disease of "busyness" and feeling overwhelmed has become a symbol of status in our culture, we are paying a high price with our quality of life and health.

We all joke around about losing our minds, but the irony is that one of the best ways to handle stress is to lose ourselves into the mind and body by way of mindfulness. The science behind mindfulness is incredible and continues to emerge. This practice allows our brain to signal to the body that all is well again, thus shutting down the emergency processes. I like to think of it as my magic stress switch. When I feel out of sorts, I know which switch will shut down the internal madness. The practice of mindfulness has created order in the chaos of my world, and trust me, no one can rock chaos like me. This knowledge I have gained and the time in practice have allowed space in my life to get quiet, centered, and process my emotions like nothing I've ever tried before.

Mindfulness practices do include breathing exercises and meditation, but it truly becomes a way of life. We try to focus on living in the present and avoid constantly dwelling on events from the past or worrying about the future. We talk about trauma and emotional baggage, which are important, but much of our stress is most likely borrowed from worry over future events that will never even happen.

It takes practice to focus on one task at a time and truly stay present in that moment. Particularly as women, we like to think that we are masters at multitasking, and while we may think we're doing great, the brain darting from task to task causes more brain fatigue than focusing on one task at the time. What? Stop multitasking? I will lose my mind for sure!

No need for panic; you can just start with small steps. The great news about mindfulness is that you can start with as little as five minutes here and there and still get great benefits. You don't need to join a monastery, sit on a rock, or change your religious views, and the benefits of meditation are limitless. They include increased happy brain chemicals, lower blood pressure, improved digestion, decreased pain, and best of all just an increased sense of peace. If we could buy all that in a pill we would race right out and get it.

It's also free and always available to you wherever you are. While I wish that my stressed out sixteen-year-old body had this gift taught to me, I am grateful for the knowledge now and for the opportunity to share with others these simple tools that make huge impacts on stress.

Resilience Skills: Mindfulness Practice

This guide can help you jumpstart your first session!

Sit in a supportive chair and rest your hands on the tops of your thighs with your legs hip distance apart

First minute: Breathe Deeply ... inhale for four counts and exhale for six counts. While focusing on the breath, think about your mind becoming quieter and feel your feet in contact with the floor.

Second minute: Tune into your breath and allow it to relax into a natural pace. Imagine the breath flowing from your shoulders to your belly. Think release.

Third minute: Continue to be aware of your breathing. If thoughts or "to do" lists enter your mind, imagine them like a cloud floating away. Don't try to push or force them out, just let them float away.

Fourth minute: Just simply sit and be; release your focus on the breath. There is nothing to fix or change ... enjoy!

Fifth minute: Think of something that you're grateful for and focus on that. Then take a moment to remember what this sensation of stillness and calm feels like. When you are ready, slowly return to your space and resume your day.

Jesus Saved Me, Dancing Healed Me

"Dance, when you're broken open. Dance, if you've torn the bandage off. Dance in the middle of the fighting. Dance in your blood. Dance when you're perfectly free."

—Rumi

DANCE BECAME MORE THAN a hobby or career; it was my coping mechanism. I have literally danced my way through some of the darkest times of my life. In my late teens and early twenties, as my home life was saturated with depression, I had a key to my dance studio. The memory of that key turning the lock, and me walking into the silence of an empty dance studio, still makes me exhale deeply a sigh of relief. This space was my refuge, and I would lock myself in and dance for hours. In that studio, I not only found peace, but I also made the final cut for the Rockettes, was crowned Miss America, and learned to believe in my dreams.

I was trained by a husband-and-wife dance team. We grew up with their children in cribs while we took class. It was very much a family atmosphere. I spent ten years under their training and two as a teacher and apprentice soaking up all I could about running a dance studio that you could never learn in school. They were my surrogate parents, and now I know they served as huge protective factors in my life. In resiliency work, a protective factor is defined as people or experiences that help people deal more effectively with stressful events and mitigate or eliminate impacts of traumatic experiences. In essence, these people or events serve as buffers against the bad events.

During these tumultuous years, like many young people, you lean on your friends. We were all just floundering through early adulthood trying to launch our ships out into the world. Though we went our separate journeys after graduation, Brent and I had forged a deep friendship in our last few years of high school. Over his years of scouting, he had become an accomplished Native American dancer. He had an insatiable drive to understand the Native American culture and a heart for the people, which I deeply admired. Though with very different styles, we loved reconnecting from time to time to share our dance journeys. I knew we had a bond that moved from school paste to super glue strength, but twenty-five years later, it has sustained beyond the grave through a bond with his family. In the summer of 1997, at the ridiculously young age of twenty-four, Brent was tragically killed. He left behind a wife, twin sons, his parents, a brother, and so many more who loved him. While his absence is felt most deeply by them, I am saddened by the brevity of our time and would have loved to share so many successes and pains with him along this crazy life. I will never hear a Don Henley song play without the need to turn up the radio and soak in the memories of his smile. At age twenty-four, it was a sobering wakeup call that life is short, and still, all these years later, there will never be on this side of heaven a good enough reason to me for this loss. God will have some explaining to do on this one.

A few months later in December, still grieving over the loss of my friend, I would dance my way through the heavy pain of my dad's death. He died in December of 1997, right at the time of the blockbuster film *Titanic* release. Thankfully, I didn't have to pay Celine Dion a royalty for every single play of "My Heart Will Go On." Hours of sweat mixed with tears allowed a physical release of the deepest pain I had known to this point in my life. As the shroud of sadness lifted, I reflected on many of his comments regarding my love for dance. As I've already shared, we didn't view the value of dance the same. I can hear him fussing as I dance down the hallway of our home: "Missy, must you dance everywhere you go?" I begin to chuckle at the fact that I should be living in that cardboard box by now because, according to Phillip, that's what happens to dance majors. Or perhaps my favorite … when he let my pageant committee know that the reason I didn't win Miss NC was because I didn't have a twirling skirt like the other girl. In the mirror I catch a glimpse of the flowing practice skirt I had put on that day in his memory and smile; his expertise was noted at least by me.

Eight years later, in my garage with three napping children, I would tap into this coping skill once again as I stumbled through postpartum depression. The transition for most women to motherhood is a huge shock to their identity, and having three kids in three-and-a-half years was way more than a transition. Your life is no longer your own. Every moment and decision revolved around the needs of three tiny humans. So to feel this one little piece and part of who I used to be was very soothing and healing.

We are all forever changed by grief, whether people or life circumstances. For me, the early losses of my dad and Brent led me to specialize in grief counseling. After experiencing it personally so early and watching so many I loved be so deeply impacted, I just naturally wanted to ease that crushing, smothering pain. I often get the remark, "I could never do your job. Isn't it so depressing to always hear about death and sadness?" I won't negate the heaviness of the work, but I'll also acknowledge the privilege of sharing this burden with people. To be allowed into another person's most inner pain and be used by God as a conduit to minister to their soul is an endowment I hope to never take for granted.

You Can't Get There from Here

> "Tell your heart that the fear of suffering is worse than the suffering itself. And that no heart has ever suffered when it goes in search of its dreams, because every second of the search is a second's encounter with God and with eternity."
>
> —Paulo Coelho, *The Alchemist*

WHEN MY HUSBAND AND I got married in 1997, I told him that he could take me anywhere in the world except Africa. No thank you. I enjoy clean running water, electricity, and nice amenities. Plus, if I want to see God's beautiful creatures like giraffes and zebras, I'll just cruise on down to the zoo, since they already brought them over for me.

Additionally, God and I had already worked this situation out way beforehand. As a young child I was one of the top fundraisers for Vacation Bible School to send missionaries all over the world. The motivation for this, my friends, was not rooted anywhere in Christian love; it was more driven by paralyzing fear. With childlike faith, I believed if I funded other people to go to these faraway places, then God would never need me to go.

Again, either God has a great sense of humor, or I didn't raise quite enough VBS funds back in the day because my first time traveling outside the United States landed my plane right on the vast continent of Africa. We interrupt your regular life program ... to take you to the one place you never wanted to go.

Like many others, I am an accidental missionary. It wasn't on my dream sheet (note that there is a recurring pattern here) to serve on the mission field in Kenya, or the US for that matter. I have always been very community-service oriented, but missionaries in my opinion were a whole level of "Holy" that I would never be on.

In 2010, I was asked to take over as the mission chair for our church. At the time I had led a few local projects already, and I was feeling energized by this work. At that point, I'd been working as a therapist for almost twelve years. I was at a point in my career where I felt like all I saw were trainwrecks daily with no solutions. To put it bluntly, I was completely burned out. I also had completely lost myself in motherhood. I no longer had a name; I was simply Landry, Jonah, and Spencer's mom.

In casting the vision for the church mission program, I felt that we needed to do programs locally, nationally, and internationally. On our journey to find programs to support internationally, my pastor invited me to meet one of his Duke Divinity School classmates who was the director of a program working with African orphans.

At the time of this meeting, I had an eight, six, and five year old, a husband, a huge caseload of clients in private practice, two cats, and a house that if not cleaned soon would likely be closed by the Wayne County Health Department. I can assure you that I rolled into the church parking lot on two wheels at two minutes past the meeting time. As I made my way to the church office, I was berating myself for the insane issue of overcommitment that I continued to struggle with. "Whatever is discussed here, I'll find someone else to lead this effort. My plate is way too full; it's someone else's turn."

After the introductions and the recollecting of the good old days by classmates, Greg began to talk about the kids the program worked with daily ... children the ages of my kids by the thousands with not only no parents to care for them but often no adults around at all. The HIV epidemic was killing so many and creating thousands of orphans a day. I was completely horrified by these thoughts. As I tried to wrap my head around it all, Greg looked at me and said, "Melissa, you should come and see for yourself; it's truly the only way to understand."

Again, even for a therapist I have a hard time holding a poker face, and I still wonder to this day what my face actually looked like. In my mind I was like, "Did he seriously just ask me to drop everything and go to Africa?" I was barely succeeding at keeping all my balls up in the air and keeping my own three kids alive here in the US. So I played the kids card. Yep, that's it, my kids were too young. To which he replied, "I have had moms travel who have kids way younger." Seriously, who are these overachiever moms who ruined my perfectly reasonable excuse? I will never be able to fully explain what happened in that room, but whatever it was, it was holy and beyond me, and I knew I was going to Africa.

There were so many rational reasons that this was *not*—I repeat, *not*—a good idea, and the fear light was blinking like a nuclear warning alert. Here is a list of just a few of the thoughts that popped like moles in my proverbial whack-a-mole brain!

What if I die? I was the mom of three young children.

What if I can't be on a plane for fourteen hours and go ballistic? I mean, do you watch the news? I could be one of those people who just loses it, plus I had only flown a few short flights, which always ended up in serious vomiting from motion sickness.

I have never traveled abroad! I had never left the US besides going to the Bahamas and that one accidental Canadian border crossing.

I don't have a passport, and if I do get one, what if I lose it and can't get home?

I'll have to get a lot of shots. I'll probably have an allergic reaction and DIE.

How will I afford it? I was self-employed and would lose two weeks of income. (Did I mention I have three kids?)

What if I contract a horrible disease?

What if I got eaten by a wild animal? For some reason, people kept reminding me of this one!

Oh … and yes … **I could DIE!**

Once I decided that I just had to do this crazy journey, I needed a partner in crime. I felt like a Girl Scout selling cookies, but instead of knocking on doors, I was literally knocking on church pew rows. People were kind and patted me on the head and commended me for being such a faithful servant of the Lord, but they were in no need of what I was peddling. God had it worked out, though, because

Lee had already been helping with fundraising, and we were an instant match. We then worked on a retired ENT doctor in our congregation. Soon the three musketeers were selected and preparing to travel.

We boarded a plane on the evening of my son's seventh birthday. Our first flight was from Raleigh to London at six hours. No problem, we were high on the excitement that was brewing. At that point I had never been on an international flight. In fact, I had never been on a flight for longer than two hours, and that had always ended in me getting seriously air sick. In London, we boarded an eight-hour flight to Nairobi. By the time we landed in Kenya, we were about to climb the walls. We spent the night in Nairobi and then set out the next morning in a van for our destination. For the record, the marking of time in Africa is a bit like being on island time. When you ask how long something takes, add a few hours to that ... OK, half a day. This few-hour ride was literally an all-day journey. At one point, Lee turned to me, pulled her sunglasses down to reveal her desperation, and said, "Melissa, you can't get there from here." Forty-eight hours of travel later as we collapsed into our beds at the final destination, there had never been a truer statement ever said.

At the time of my first mission trip, the children and youth we met during our stay were participating in an empowerment program offered through ZOE Empowers (zoeempowers.org). The program uses a unique model that keeps orphans and vulnerable children living with their families while moving out of poverty in just three years. Rather than building schools or offering medical services, the purpose of this type of mission experience is to connect and build relationships.

Day after day, we would sit circled around together and listen as one by one each child would tell their story of how they came into the program. Most of the children were either total orphans or vulnerable children taking care of sick relatives. A large majority had watched their parents die of HIV and then been disgracefully shunned by their own relatives and communities after their deaths. As if this wasn't enough, most of them had endured some type of work exploitation, physical abuse, and/or sexual abuse.

As I listened to the kids that were near the end of the three-year program share their stories, the first thing that struck me was the way they labeled their tragedies. Instead of using words like "troubles," they used the word "challenges." Confidently they would say "I once had challenges, like the death of my parents and no food to eat, but I found hope and a new way to move forward."

As a therapist, I couldn't even think how in such a short amount of time these kids could arrive at this place of emotional peace. So just like that, the teacher became the student.

In spite of all the initial fear, I didn't die. In fact, I became more alive than I had ever been. That one *yes*, that one toe in the water, opened an entire door in my life that would have forever remained locked if I'd let fear win out. I can't imagine my life without saying yes to that moment. Because of that one yes, an entire sequence of events unfolded that I never could have dreamed. I see the whole world in new ways and found my truest self and calling.

Sweet Stella, Sunscreen, and Swahili

"After he had washed their feet, had put on his robe, and had returned to the table, he said to them, "Do you know what I have done to you? You call me Teacher and Lord—and you are right, for that is what I am. So if I, your Lord and Teacher, have washed your feet, you also ought to wash one another's feet. For I have set you an example, that you also should do as I have done to you"

(John 13:12–15)

THE ONLY WAY TO truly know what other people need is to listen to their hearts. We do a lot of assuming about what we think other people need or want. To truly understand what people want or need, we must listen. My time in Kenya really cemented this in my brain. I thought that attempting to learn a few phrases in Swahili would be a great way to connect. It only led to serious giggles followed by, "Melissa, we wish to speak English."

There are also many things we take for granted because of our perspective that we assume others will know. As we sat circled up outside in the hot African sun, I reached into my backpack and pulled out my sunscreen and began to slather the 100 lotion over my lily-white skin. As I placed it back in my bag, I noticed that I had become quite the novelty act of the moment. Faith, one of the teens sitting by me, leaned over and asked, "What is that?" I told her it was sunscreen to prevent me from getting burned by the sun. Within seconds, the whisper passed around the circle like the old game of telephone whispered ear to ear. Then heads nodded with smiles, as if the understanding had been reached and we were now free to continue the meeting.

The question I was most frequently asked after returning from Kenya was, "What did you do there?" People seemed really upset when I said, "We met with the kids, listened to their journey, and shared fellowship." If this was a post on social media, I feel that I would get a thumbs down. While I certainly value evidenced based research and what it brings to our practices, I've always been more drawn to the things that are indeed beyond measure. It's difficult to measure changes deep in people's souls, or the impact of hope or faith on their lives. When and if I participate in research, I'm a qualitative girl all the way. I love to sit down and interview people and conduct focus groups. Maybe I'm channeling my inner journalist, but I didn't need stratified random samples or data to know that someone's life had been changed.

I think we must be careful in our lives that we don't get consumed by numbers but rather are more concerned with the heart of people. As mothers we feel the numbers pressure from day one. Is your baby walking by twelve months? Are they talking? How old were they when they read? … SAT scores, and the hits roll on. We must remember that these are all guidelines, and while we should take heed and concern at times, for the most part kids are just kids.

In our personal lives, what numbers rule us? The scale, our financial worth, the number of likes on social media? In our churches, how do we evaluate our programs—by numbers or heart value? Do we judge or evaluate others based on numbers rather than the heart?

One of the most poignant events occurred when our team went to the home of a young girl named Stella. Like so many kids in the ZOE program, Stella's parents were deceased, and she was caring for her younger siblings. She had a table prepared for us, and as we sat at the table, she proceeded to lovingly wash our hands with a pitcher of water. For a follower of Christ, it was as if I'd been touched by Jesus. It was one of the most beautiful moments of my life.

This young girl, not much older than my own daughter, who just a few months before had been begging for her next meal on the street due to the death of her parents, was now sharing what she had with complete strangers. Somehow Stella and her peers had learned not only to say, "Life may not always be going the way I think it should ... but I am going to be ok," but they also lived with deep gratitude for what they were blessed with each day.

In my innocence as a new mission worker, I had been excited for this opportunity to go help these "poor, needy" children in Kenya. Unbeknownst to me, along with my lofty hopes and dreams to help, I carried with me a lifetime of stereotypes and stigma that were being shattered wide open each day. Not only were my beliefs and attitudes rocked to my core, but no less by a group of teenagers who had no running water, electricity, and ... GASP ... no advanced college degrees!

In our success-oriented, consumer-driven culture, we're led to believe that nothing bad should ever happen to us and that happiness can be found in the next thing we achieve or purchase. Living under this very narrow and false pretense creates unrealistic expectations and sets us up for failure. It's not realistic to believe that only good things will happen to us and that we will never face challenges, yet this is marketed to us every day.

If we're willing to let go of these false beliefs and replace them with more realistic thoughts, we can build something important for our brains, called margin. This created space of margin allows our brain to process more than one outcome to a situation, thereby allowing for more than one solution. Margin is way more than having a Plan B; it's allowing for the possibility of multiple things to occur. When we hold rigid black and white beliefs about what should happen or should not happen in our lives, it only leads to disappointment.

Remember that resilience doesn't have to mean we live what is happening, but we do accept that things are different. Just as Stella had to accept the loss of her parents and her new responsibilities, things may not go the way you originally planned, but knowing you'll be OK despite these challenges goes a long way.

Resilience Skill: Gratitude

Practicing gratitude in our lives is a great way to help us daily build resiliency. Find things to be thankful for and focus on those rather than your disappointments. You can write them out in your journal or name them throughout the day,

Never Judge a Book, or a Child by Its Cover

"If I was a book, I would like to be a library book, so I would be taken home by all different sorts of kids."

—Cornelia Funke

I LOVE BOOKS. I fell in love with books before I even knew how to read. Maybe it's because of my mom's promise of a new Golden book for good behavior during grocery shopping, but whatever the reason, the passion for reading has always been there. I know that part of my confidence as a woman lies in the hours of time I spent reading biographies of trailblazing women like Clara Barton, Florence Nightingale, and Elizabeth Blackwell. I instantly connected with their strong spirits and the need to do good in the world. I don't even need to read it—just the possession of those crisp pages makes me feel like I possess the knowledge that's held between the covers.

After returning home from Kenya, I set back into my comfortable routine of carpool, laundry, work, and the million other mom tasks that consumed my days. It would have been easy to say, "Well, I did my part," pat myself on the back, and get back to my reality. Alas, even amidst the busyness I couldn't erase the faces I had seen or quieten the voices I had heard. I continued to feel an incredible burden to share the stories of these children beyond just telling my friends and family. People needed to know that all over the world children were trying to live without parents, and that programs like ZOE Empowers needed their support to make a difference.

I was, in fact, "gloriously ruined." This is a term I learned from Kay Warren, Pastor Rick Warren's wife. Those who have traveled to places of extreme poverty or devastation know exactly what I'm talking about. For me, this term refers to the wrestling and flood of emotions that I encountered as I tried to understand the injustice of what I had witnessed against the backdrop of my now incredibly apparent affluence.

For the first time in my life, I had to try to sort out how I was going to deal with living in a society of excess knowing firsthand that others are struggling daily just to meet the basic needs of life. Sure, I'm a counselor and had read and studied about extreme poverty in the US and abroad, but now for me poverty had names and faces attached. I would lie awake at night thinking about what if those were my children crying out in starvation. My Jonah, my Spencer, and my Landry; I would want someone to fight for them.

My trip also made me painfully aware of the amount of privilege our children were being raised in daily. I desired for my children to not only know how incredibly blessed their lives were, but I also felt that somehow they could be a part of the solution.

Like many parents over the years, we had tried to instill compassion into our children through various avenues. Often that included reading them books about people whose lives looked different than theirs. I decided that a children's book for ZOE could help highlight not only the dire problems with orphans but also this incredible model that was transforming their lives.

After getting the green light from the ministry to try this idea, my mind set into motion like the Mad Hatter running to the tea party! Well, not exactly. I had always secretly dreamed of writing a children's book, but I truly had no idea what I was doing! So I did what every book-addicted, aspiring writer does ... I researched and read everything I could on writing for children. (Note: I may also have googled "How to write a children's book.")

Then there was this nagging problem called *time*. Any mom with young children knows all too well that you never have time to do the things you want, so you must find it. Most aspiring writers have lofty notions of spilling out words onto the page in a nice, quiet coffee shop. Well, maybe that worked for Hemingway but not for this working mom of three. I wrote and edited waiting in pick-up lines, waiting for practices to end, and waiting for pots of noodles to boil. Basically, anywhere I could, and I assure you it was anything but quiet! God began to write this story in my heart, and trust me when I say He would not let me put it away.

After creating what I thought was the best children's book since Dr. Suess wrote *Green Eggs and Ham*, I submitted my final draft to the ZOE staff. I obsessively check my inbox waiting for the reply that said, "Yes, let's do this!" However, the response was not at all what I expected, and to be truthful, it brought me to tears. ZOE could not use the story I had created, and I was heartbroken, but it wasn't for the reasons you might think.

In my efforts to create a story that children could relate to, the original version of the book used personification, with whimsical talking animals relaying the plight of the children and the work of ZOE. I was unaware that in the early years of the organization, ZOE spent a great deal of time educating people that African children were not synonymous with animals. A difficult concept for many of us to grasp, but it was a reality. I just couldn't wrap my mind around the fact that any child could be perceived as less than human. I seriously sobbed for an entire day.

Take heart, my parenting friends who are in the throes of raising strong-willed children—this is when being a strong-willed child serves you well in life. I remembered my lessons on resiliency and was supported by the idea that if these children could overcome all those challenges, then I could persevere. In fact, this just fueled my fire to create a book that not only relayed the story of the program but would ensure these children were portrayed in their true humanity.

The idea of paralleling Stella's day with an American child her age became the new storyline. Initially in the story process, Stella was the oldest child in her family, just like the true Stella. During a writing revision session with another writer, I was encouraged to not make Stella the head of the family. Given the heavy topics such as the death of parents, and all the challenges the children would face in the story, it was best that children perceived that the main character had someone to champion for her. The character of Caroline was added to be her older sister and fulfill that purpose.

A children's book is nothing without illustrations, so enter the one and only Amy Burkhardt Fetzer! I always say that Amy is the yen to my yang. I'm the most hyperactive, high strung, Type A person you could ever meet. Counter that with the coolest, most Zen Yoga teacher ever, and there is Amy. I'm still in awe that a mother of three would take six months out of her life with no financial compensation to lovingly draw this artwork. Years later, I still get emotional just typing these words. This woman loves Jesus!

The incredible beauty about Amy's work is the prayer and heart she puts into each piece of her art. She has never traveled to Kenya or met the children she brought to life, but when I saw her initial images, I was instantly transported to Kenya. Her humble spirit and love for people flowed from her hands and into her art as she brought the children to life on the pages of the book.

The book was printed, and we all lived happily ever after. Yeah, not so fast. The next step was publishing. This became a whole new adventure of exploring self-publishing versus traditional publishing, and I will waste no space on this debate here, as this topic already has countless blogs and books dedicated to it. We chose to self-publish because, given the purpose of the book, we wanted to maintain 100 percent artistic control. To self-publish we also had to use Crowd Sourcing to fund the process, and we were blown away by the generosity of so many.

If I had to sum up this process in a sentence it would be the old adage, "You Can't Judge a Book by Its Cover." Until now, no one really knew all that went into creating *Elizabeth and Stella Meet ZOE*, or any other book for that matter. Likewise, we never truly know what has gone into creating the story that makes up the life of a person; we just see the outward cover. We don't usually think about the joys, challenges, and sorrows they have experienced; unfortunately, we just make a quick judgment based on appearances, especially in this age of social media. I wonder just how much more peace we could bring into our world and lives if we stopped to make this one little change of truly getting to know the whole person.

Journal: Slaying Fear

What is one of your goals or desires? Don't let fear stop you from taking this step or your next life step. Take some time to reflect and write down your goals and what steps need to happen to realize this plan. Whatever your life plan, even if it gets reworked, just like this book, you might wind up with a better version than you ever dreamed!

Achievement

My Isaac Moment

"*After these things God tested Abraham. He said to him, 'Abraham!' And he said, 'Here I am.' He said, 'Take your son, your only son Isaac, whom you love, and go to the land of Moriah, and offer him there as a burnt offering on one of the mountains that I shall show you'*"

(Genesis 22:1–2)

IN MAY OF 2015, I pondered this in my journal:

> *The saying goes, "Why would anyone want to jump out of a perfectly good airplane?" Well, that is exactly what I feel like I am about to do. After struggling for so long spiritually and emotionally, I have such a peace that God is calling me out of private practice, never out of counseling, but He has something greater for me—but I have to be willing to jump out of this perfect airplane and leave the safety I know. But is it really as safe as I think? What if my airplane is on autopilot and headed right for a mountain? I am so confirmed that this is the right path. I pray for balance and the ability to hold fast even in the hard times.*

Even before I became a parent, hearing the chilling account of Abraham placing his son on an altar to be sacrificed made me know that I could never have that kind of faith. Well, we all have Issacs in our lives, and they're not always our children. They can be all kinds of things. For me, my practice had become my Isaac. Not that I worshiped it, but it was my identity and security blanket. I had worked so hard to build a strong reputation and deliver the best care. I had spent years in school and even longer perfecting my craft. Who was I and where would I work without this business?

In January of 2015, as a part of this calling, I started working on my Master of Public Health. Yet another area of my life that I never sought out, as it found me (aka God put me here). My life plan on my Pinterest vision board had me completing my PhD in counseling and spending the next half of my career teaching others how to help others. Yes, I would use my experience and pain to help others. Now doesn't that sound noble?

Yet again, God had other plans. Since becoming involved in international mission work in 2012, my interest in global health had been piqued. If you ever wondered who orders textbooks on global health and infectious disease and reads them for fun ... that would be me. The thing that sold me the most on public and global health was just how life changing information and practices that I took for granted were. The basic principles such as clean water and hand hygiene could change the health of so many.

While we live in a time when it's not uncommon for students to return to school at any age, I have to say returning to school in your forties, with three kids, a private practice ... oh yes, and twenty years since you accessed a university library (where the heck are the card catalogs?) was more than intimidating.

Even though it was certainly full of "I am going to quit" moments, I loved my time in public health school. It was like pulling the curtain back and finding the answers that you had an inkling were there all along, but you just never knew quite where to look or how to define it.

One of the unexpected blessings out of this time that I never counted on were my classmates. Even though I was old enough to be most of their moms, they were so amazing, and I treasure the connection to many of them today. What I lacked in tech skills and modern day learning they gladly taught me, and with great encouragement. They also valued my years of real-world experience and were hungry to learn about mental health. Their interaction and reception of me was always confirming of this call, which often needed a lot of reassurance.

The roadblocks came up from day one of orientation. It was a cold January day, and the rain was relentless—a freaking African monsoon falling in Eastern North Carolina. I had an hour commute and a babysitting mix up, as I was still homeschooling my youngest two children. I remember driving in the pouring rain and thinking, *What am I doing? I've already done all this and have my "big girl" degree*. It simultaneously felt so insane and so right at the same time. That's how you know when you're in the will of God—when you know that if you could have your own free will and just stop because *you* don't need this, then it's probably of God.

At orientation, one of the big take-aways is that in order to complete the MPH degree, you have to write a professional level research paper with the intent of professional publication. I assured my advisor that I would not be doing two things. First, I would not be researching or writing on mental health topics. Nope. Remember, I'm in recovery from that career. Also, I wouldn't be conducting any primary research. Nope. I was going to allow myself to underachieve here. Let me research heart disease, diabetes, strokes, anything but mental health. Oh, but be careful what you tell the universe that you are *not* going to do.

Turning Points

"We are afflicted in every way, but not crushed; perplexed, but not driven to despair; persecuted, but not forsaken; struck down, but not destroyed"

(2 Corinthians 4:8–9)

IT WAS THREE WEEKS before my graduation from MPH school, and I was stressed to the max. I was preparing to present my research to faculty, which ironically enough was on ... yep, wait for it ... mental health. ACEs, to be exact, and the connection to physical health. I was also preparing for multiple finals and closing out my private practice. Oh yes, and I had kids somewhere in there. With all the whirlwind of stress, I really didn't have time to process all these big changes in my life.

I started my private practice journey in 2001 in a group practice. Many of my colleagues had big dreams of opening their own practice, but not me. I was perfectly happy to see my people and do my thing. In 2011, I was forced by circumstances to open my own. It was scary, but I grew so much from the experience. It was like birthing a child. I named it, designed the space and logos, and built it from the ground up. Now here I was six years later about to close this chapter of my life. Funny how the grief counselor doesn't recognize her own losses.

On Good Friday, Sadie Jane came by my office to help me pack up my things. As we were working, she was telling me about a job that a colleague was looking to fill. I really wasn't interested, as I had decided that I needed a break. I was going to take the summer to look for a job in public health and spend time with my kids.

The workaholic in me was feeling guilty about not bringing money in, so I decided to talk with someone about the job. I would be supervising eight crisis counselors who were working to assist survivors rebuild after Hurricane Matthew. Ok, I had never supervised anyone other than my kids, and I didn't know crap about disaster recovery. I told her to give me the weekend and I would let her know.

That Sunday was Easter Sunday, and I was preparing for the usual family festivities. Since the birth of our children, Easter Sunday had been church and lunch at our home. I'm one of those sick people who actually enjoys cooking and entertaining. Cooking is very therapeutic for me. With so many of my family members gone, I know I feel close to them in the kitchen, especially on holidays.

One of the upsides of having a teen mom is that you get to experience family members. I had significant time with not only my grandmas but also my great grandmothers. Interesting, though, I had no experiences with granddads.

That Saturday after my morning cooking escapade, my husband and I went to complete packing up my office. He just rushed in and was throwing things in boxes like he just couldn't get out of there fast enough. I don't even know what triggered it, but we got into a huge fight. I know now that I was needing that moment to just acknowledge and grieve the close of this chapter. While he had no idea, he was just dismissing all my work.

That night I was a mess. I barely slept, and I just went back and forth about what to do with the job. I got up the next morning, dressed, and got my kids ready for church. My husband had to be at the early service to run the sound, so the kids and I were going to the 11:00 service. On the drive to church I felt like I couldn't stay; I had to go. I didn't know how I was going to sit through church or a meal. I didn't know where I was going, but I had to get away.

I dropped my kids off and texted my husband that I wasn't coming and didn't know when I'd be back. I ran home, changed my clothes, and got in my car. Where was I going? This was it; I was finally having a breakdown. I wondered how many years it would take. Yep, apparently forty-four.

I decided on Little Washington, a small town on the Pamlico River. I have several runaway places in North Carolina, and this has become one of them.

I parked and began to walk around this historic town. Church services were out and for the most part it was deserted and quiet. Almost every church had a white shroud draped from a wooden cross blowing in the breeze to symbolize the risen Lord. I felt a peace and holy presence, but I also wondered if I was a bad mom for leaving my kids on a holiday.

I walked through the local cemeteries. I love history, and nothing grounds me quicker than a stroll through an old cemetery and reading the tombstones. Even though they're not here, to feel connected to others before my time is an incredible feeling for me. Note that at forty-four I had outlived most of these people. I recognized that life is fleeing and asked myself what I really wanted out of this next chapter in my life.

I wrote this in my journal while sitting:

I have come away to Be Still and hope to hear confirmation from the Lord on the next steps. For the last 2.5 years, I have been working so hard to finish this degree. I am 100 confident that this was God's plan for me. As I have come to the end now, trying to find the place that God wants to use me has become very overwhelming. I have certainly been fine with God using me and me being willing to serve in any capacity, even if it means a local health department. But as I sift through what is of God and what is not, I do know that God's calling in my life involves global health. He has not called me to work only in the local health dept. I feel my long-term place is in medical missions, and I just have to keep preparing myself. The opportunity to work at Easter Seals UCP with this FEMA program that has just presented itself seems like a lot of positive professional work that would help increase my skills in supervision and admin, which I will need to work in a global NGO. Plus, God is giving me an opportunity to do this and be present in this season for my kids and family. So why hesitate? Because I am tired. These last 6 years have just been pushing from one thing to the next, and I really wanted a break. For once, I want off the Merry Go Round.

Disaster Recovery Round One

"Seek first to understand, then to be understood."

—Steven Covey

IF YOU OPEN YOURSELF up to the will of God, you better be ready for anything, and I mean anything. On Friday, May 5, 2017, I walked across the stage for graduation, and on Monday, May 8, I started my job with the FEMA crisis counseling program. This program was a complete 180 from everything I had ever known. It used a community health worker model, which I was comfortable with in public health but leery of as a mental health therapist.

The Crisis Counseling Program (CCP) is a federally funded US program that can be awarded to states post-disaster with the hopes of mitigating the mental health impacts of the event. So often after disasters people think of the physical needs of people, but the emotional impacts are huge as well. In our program, each county we covered was served by a team of two crisis counselors who were responsible for covering the entire county. Remember, this is rural North Carolina, which means you can drive miles without seeing anything but fields. They would spend their days literally driving door to door to talk with survivors. We battled the line daily between being case managers and mental health workers. It was often blurry.

Most of my staff had four-year degrees in social work or psychology, and a few either had or were working on master's degrees. I was comfortable with the level of what they were asked to do up to a certain point, and then the thought of a non-licensed person "assessing" for mental health issues disturbed me. Within the first week of being in my position, I made the egregious error of making such a comment to our regional supervisor in front of my staff. Apparently, I had forgotten my own lesson to listen first and engage my mouth much later. I was immediately put in my place by one of my staff, who let me know very sternly that while she may not have all those fancy degrees, she knew her community and her skill set, and she was offended by my condescending attitude. Yet more confirmation that people in their own communities know what they need better than an outsider, no matter the level of education or experience. Rest assured, I will not make that mistake ever again.

My work with the crisis counseling program for survivors of Hurricane Matthew, which was called HOPE for NC, turned out to be one of the greatest experiences of my career. This experience tested, stretched, and grew me like no other professional experience ever. There is nothing anyone can teach you in school or training that can prepare you to sit eye to eye with another human being who has lost literally everything but their life. It's increasingly difficult to counsel with those who have lost everything for the second go around. I was more often the student than teacher in this job for sure. In the end, rather than feeling that more experienced professionals were needed, I viewed this program as what should be the standard for mental health work. We should be training more everyday community people to administer this information, just like we encourage as many people as possible to know CPR. We should all have basic mental health first aid skills.

I Only Iron For Jesus

"But take care and watch yourselves closely, so as neither to forget the things that your eyes have seen nor to let them slip from your mind all the days of your life; make them known to your children and your children's children"

(Deuteronomy 4:9)

PANTIES AND PERIODS, CERTAINLY not anything that I ever thought would make me an international sensation. Like most young girls of my time, I had at times imagined myself walking down the runway and being the next Cindy Crawford. However, modeling underwear in a foreign country seemed a very suspect way to show the love of Jesus. Yet here I was showing women how to put reusable liners in their underwear.

The first rule of health education is to assume that the person knows nothing. Start at zero. Despite a degree in public health, I had never once stopped to think of what other women do in other countries for their monthly cycles, or the health and mental implications of suffering from what is referred to as period poverty.

In the winter of 2017, I was, as my teenagers would say, "all up in my feelings." It was my last semester of graduate school, and I had multiple papers due, mother guilt, wife guilt, and quite possibly was on my last pair of clean underwear. With all this swirling about, I had been invited to a small church in Snow Hill, North Carolina to see a project called "Days for Girls." All I knew going into this was that a small group of people came together twice a month to make feminine hygiene kits for a mission trip. Did I mention they meet early on Saturday mornings in the cold of winter? Oh, but yes, please, please, and I do mean please, sign me up. Who knew that this one act of getting up when I didn't want to, putting aside my pressing needs, and taking those first steps would open a door to a life-changing adventure?

As I walked through the fellowship hall doors that morning, the scent of a hot iron touching new fabric and of coffee transported me back to my great-grandmother's quilting room and my great aunt's sewing room, both places where I had experienced safety and love as a child. It was like I was instantly enveloped in the hug of their spirits that said, "You are home." I was warmly welcomed, and since I have zero sewing skills besides sewing ribbons onto pointe shoes, I was given the job to iron the fabric. I hate to iron, so here I was doing something I loathe early on a Saturday morning but loving every minute of it. Hence the phrase, "I only iron for Jesus."

What was going on in this small, rural fellowship hall was incredible. Various people gathered in love to create safe, washable kits for women living over three thousand miles away whom they would never meet. These weren't "some people." These were true disciples of Christ. In this room, the hands of seasoned women, young women, children, farmers, and brothers worked to sew, cut, and piece together these kits that would allow women to stay in school or go to their jobs each month as they experienced their menstrual cycle. The educational and economic impact for these girls and women who miss school or work due to their cycles runs deep.

These worker bees are fueled by the sobering knowledge that one in ten girls in Sub Sahara Africa, 113 million adolescent girls in India, and 30 percent of menstruating girls in rural Brazil will miss school this year due to lack of feminine hygiene products (daysforgirls.org). To try to manage, they often use whatever they can find, such as banana leaves, mattress stuffing, or even cow dung, to control their flow. This leads to increased risk of infection and possible long-term damage to girls and women.

I had no idea that this simple day would open my life up to even more incredible opportunities. In August of 2017, I traveled with the team to rural Guatemala to educate and distribute these kits. We would roll up early in the morning on the chicken bus to find sometimes hundreds of women and girls lined up at the clinic to attend the class and receive the kit. It was like Black Friday shopping on steroids for free menstrual kits. Teaching the classes was so eye-opening—just to know how little exposure and education these women had on the way their bodies worked. Knowing that some of this was intentional in suppressing women in this culture was simultaneously infuriating. It was so rewarding to be able to ease their fears about what was normal and abnormal related to menstruation, and to teach them how take care of their monthly needs in a way to prevent infection and save precious resources. It was priceless. This shared time together was also a beautiful reminder of how much we have in common as women, even though we look and conduct life in different ways. There is power when women come together in connection. Take note, men.

I also worked alongside an inspiring team of medical providers, including a marvelous nurse practitioner named Dell. As I watched her work with compassion and wisdom, I would listen to cases and try to diagnose along in my head. She has a daughter who is a mental health professional, so she placed high value on our work. So many women would come in with what we call psychosomatic complaints: headaches, heartburn, referred pains. These are true symptoms but are often caused by psychological stressors.

Dell would look at me and say, "She's all yours." At first it was very intimidating. I had never counseled outside the US. While I've always tried to be very sensitive about culture and had just completed advanced studies in ethnic health disparities, what did I really know about the struggles of these women? They walked miles to get water and grew their own food for an entire family, all with children strapped to their backs. I felt they should be teaching me how to be less entitled.

Then there was the issue of working through a translator. How would this impact the rapport building that is the backbone of counseling. One thing I had learned from my postpartum counseling groups was that no matter the socioeconomic situation, motherhood is universal. So I started where I felt comfortable.

Me: Hola, my name is Melissa. I have three children.

I pause for translation.

Me: How many children do you have?

I pause to wait for translation

Mom: Seis (6)

Me: Wow, that must be exhausting.

As Arlete translates, the mom rapidly shakes her head.

Mom: Si, si.

Me: I bet you just want to run and hide sometimes.

Before Arlete can complete her translations, this mom is laughing and smiling as she says, "Si, si."

I smile at her, barriers broken. We are just two moms who get it; raising children is stressful no matter the nationality. I would share breathing techniques and grounding skills, things that she could use long after our team was a distant memory.

This trip just confirmed my calling to medical missions, and I felt that I needed to complete my circle with more clinical skills. I began to wrestle with the idea of getting my RN degree. Was this the time to pursue that goal that had been parked at age twenty to allow for my dance pursuit? How could I go to school again? What is wrong with me? Is it that I just can't be satisfied, or is it a real calling? All I knew to do was what I'd been doing for the last few years: journal, pray, and put one foot in front of the other.

Return to the Wilderness

"Surely the Lord your God has blessed you in all your undertakings; he knows your going through this great wilderness. These forty years the Lord your God has been with you; you have lacked nothing"

(Deuteronomy 2:7)

INSPIRED BY MY WORK in Guatemala and with the encouragement of my team, I decided to open my mind to returning to RN school. I enrolled in an EMT course at the local community college to increase my basic skills and to ensure it was what I really wanted to do. Every Tuesday and Thursday evening from six to ten I attended class and soaked up every skill they could throw at us. It was so refreshing after writing paper after paper in graduate school because I was doing hands-on procedures, and it was fantastic. I was living the dream channeling my *Emergency!* days for real.

After the CCP disaster program ended in December of 2017, I started applying for jobs a few months before our grant expired. I applied for anything and everything related to public health and poverty alleviation. At one point I had applied to over forty positions—everything from a health educator in the local health department to executive director of nonprofits. March of 2018 rolled around, and I still didn't have a full-time job. I was absolutely shocked that with all my education and years of experience I was unemployed. I was branded as a therapist, and it seemed that no one could see me outside of that box. I have never understood being "overqualified." If you're willing to do the work and accept the pay, who cares?

This was a very dark and discouraging time for me and reminiscent of my time in the wilderness from burnout several years earlier. I became extremely depressed and angry at God. I felt like I had worked so hard and been willing to walk away from so much, and now I was unemployed. I've always worked several jobs or been in school. I didn't know what to do with myself. The lack of routine coupled with the unknown of the future wreaked havoc on my anxiety. My drinking became problematic, and I was completely disengaged from my family. I have struggled off and on in my life with severe insomnia, but this was the absolute worst. I would fall asleep for a few hours and then was awake until five or six in the morning. I'd take my kids to school, work out, and then just try to fill that time. Many nights I would just lie on my floor and cry. Even with therapy and several medication changes, I felt hopeless. No one could encourage me; they all meant well, but in my eyes, I was a failure.

Desperate to alleviate my depression, I decided to view this time as a gift to work on my writing. I had wanted to seriously write for several years, but other pursuits had captured my time. Since I couldn't find a job that targeted what I felt called to do, I created my own social entrepreneurship: Resiliency Counseling and Consulting, PLLC (RCC). I wanted to create more than a business. I wanted to create a movement related to resilience. I hoped to lead seminars on the biology of resilience and teach coping skills. I started blogging about mental health prevention and the normalization of mental health issues.

Anyone who has launched a business knows that you initially spend money, and it takes a while to generate revenue, so I still needed a source of real income. I approached my long-term colleague about joining her practice and began seeing clients in her office that spring. It was a humbling experience because it felt like going backwards. This was so not what I wanted to be doing, but the bills needed to be paid, and I was grateful to have the opportunity. As we moved through the summer, I continued to apply for jobs and build my therapy client caseload.

In August of 2018, I returned to Guatemala for a second adventure. This trip just deepened my calling to medical missions, as I was able to put my EMT skills to use in the clinic. I continued to lead health education and worked with Dell in the clinic. Our team worked so well integrating the mental, physical, and spiritual into healthcare. It made me so discouraged to return to work in the US to a system that saw mental and physical health so separately. If this team could get the concept in a developing country with little resources, why didn't we get it as a system? Weren't we supposed to be so advanced?

I still felt this incredible spiritual burden that made me wrestle with thoughts of either selling everything and following Jesus, or possibly checking myself into a local mental facility for evaluation. No matter what, I needed resolution and desperately wanted to figure out where I was supposed to be. I reached out to several pastors and mentors who knew my heart and my calling, and this was where I learned about a special community in the United Methodist Church called Deaconess and Home Missioners (DHM).

My journey to becoming a deaconess, like most spiritual discernments, was a twisty and winding path. Maybe a few called to our community knew someone and wanted to emulate that. Most of us who were called to this role found that we didn't fit into traditional church roles. We were a bit like the toys on the Island of Misfit Toys. We had a sincere capacity to serve but didn't fit traditional roles. After completing my MPH, I knew I felt called to serve in health equities, but finding this place was a daunting task.

Deaconesses and Home Missioners are laywomen and laymen who are called by God to be in a lifetime relationship in The United Methodist Church. We dedicate our vocations to serve in ministries of love, justice, and service. We form a covenant community that together we strive to alleviate suffering, eradicate causes of injustice, facilitate the development of full human potential, and share in building global community as the church universal. I like to joke that we're the nuns of the Methodist church, with the freedom to marry and wear normal clothing. I was accepted into candidacy, and I was eager to begin my classes and this journey. Not so fast … Mother Nature, AKA God, had other plans.

Disaster Recovery Round Two

*"Though Satan should buffet, though trials should come
Let this blest assurance control
That Christ has regarded my helpless estate
And has shed His own blood for my soul"*

—Horatio Spafford

IN SEPTEMBER OF 2018 in Eastern North Carolina, we sat for weeks watching Hurricane Florence slowly crawl towards us. I was so fearful that the communities we'd just assisted to recover from Matthew would be under water again. It eventually made landfall near Wrightsville Beach, North Carolina. Record rainfalls of over twenty inches in some areas, and as I had feared, many of the same towns under water two years ago from Matthew were suffering again.

I wasn't surprised to be called to work as a shelter-based crisis counselor for those who had been forced to leave their homes. At one point the flooding was so bad that for me to get to the shelter I was going to have to be ferried by boat. After my FEMA experience, I said, *"I got this."* I mean, come on, in addition to all this fancy education, I've been in this fray before. So feeling prepared for this challenge, I packed my mental health backpack with bubbles, balloons, coloring supplies, and was off to save the world.

If you've never been inside of a shelter during a natural disaster, it's like stepping into another world. By the time I arrived, many of the people had been there since the first bands of the storm rolled in on Thursday, and it was now Tuesday. Six days away from home and as wonderful as the staff and volunteers can try, this is certainly not a luxury vacation: cots lined up as far as the eye can see, a sea of people, children running around, and in general ... just organized chaos.

As I worked my way around the room, I naturally gravitated to the children. I chatted with them about how they were doing, and we would pull out bubbles or crayons and play. Most of them were oblivious to the severity of the situation. They just knew that a big storm came and now they were safe. At that moment, true to children, the contents of my bag were way more important than the storm.

As they giggled and asked to braid my hair, my heart sank as I thought of how many of their schools were likely damaged. On top of losing their homes, their schools were also under water. I knew the impact on the education for many children in Eastern North Carolina would be gravely impacted by this storm. A natural disaster is most definitely an adverse childhood experience. My public health brain also knew that after large storms like Florence, there would be many educational impacts. Students could lose an entire year of their education, resulting in a huge increase in retention rates, not to mention the emotional ramifications of living in multiple places. Disproportionately, the impact would be amongst those of lower socioeconomic status and children of color due to property value and housing in the flood plain. The same kids who already struggled to keep up in school and life would suffer yet another setback before they could even begin. Suddenly I didn't feel as confident as I had initially when I entered the room. Actually, I felt a little sick.

As I worked around the room, I saw Betty (name changed for confidentiality) and asked her if I could sit down and talk with her. She shared with me where she lived and what brought her to the shelter. I listened as she talked about flying for the first time in her life in a helicopter ... that would be the military one that rescued her and her husband as the waters rose.

As if this harrowing experience wasn't enough, this was the third flood Betty and her husband have endured in their life together. Twice they have rebuilt their home, and she feared it was about to happen again. During our time together, Betty's husband, George (name changed for confidentiality) came and sat down beside her. It was evident by their interaction that there was a deep love and bond between them. This was a couple that had been through a lot together, and I had just scratched the surface.

I asked Betty how they were able to find the strength to rebuild time and time again. I told her I felt like I would just give up. She said, *"You can't give up; you have to press on."* She told me that sometimes she feels like giving up and says, *"God, why me?"* And God answers her with, *"Why not you?"*

Wow! As I was attempting to process how I could have that kind of attitude about life, that's when she dropped the next bomb in my lap. As if the loss of her home multiple times wasn't enough to send someone into a lifetime of depression, Betty and George had just lost their daughter less than two months before Hurricane Florence. Their daughter had a chronic illness that had led to paralysis and finally took her life.

That's when I realized the tables were turning and, yet again, the counselor was becoming the counselee. I had walked into this space with a brain full of diagnostic skills, therapy tools, and public health knowledge, but nothing could trump what Betty and George already knew: adversity creates resiliency. The truth is this lady was probably more psychologically ready to handle this level of event than I or most people I know. As I continued to listen to her reminisce about her daughter and what she missed, an old hymn came to mind. I told Betty that her attitude and spirit reminded me of the hymn "It Is Well with My soul" and asked her if she knew the story about the person who wrote the hymn.

We discussed how Horatio Spafford (full disclosure: at the time, neither of us could recall his name) wrote this particular hymn after losing his four daughters at sea; only his wife survived. After the accident at sea, he received a telegram that said, "Saved alone." It's reported that he wrote the words to the beloved hymn as the ship he was on to reunite with his wife passed over the spot where his daughters died. *Have mercy*, I can't imagine the power of the human spirit in that moment.

Betty said, *"People think I'm crazy because I tell them I hear God talking to me, but I do."* After her daughter died, she said the Lord told her to be grateful for the years she'd had her daughter and the blessing of the four children she still had. Of course, she misses her and grieves, but what an incredible perspective.

Thankfully for my family and many others, Florence was just an interruption in our lives. We lost some days of work and school to prepare and shelter. After the storm, some of us endured days without power and probably a little bit too much family togetherness. As frustrating and overwhelming as all of this was, they were just that ... interruptions. Just like that, many of us were back to zipping around town, our kids in school or returning soon, and we were living at the mercy of that busy calendar again.

But for so many like Betty or the children I met, Florence wasn't just an interruption of their lives; it was complete devastation. Some families suffered the ultimate loss—the loss of life. Not only have many lost their homes and all their possessions in the historical flood waters, but they lost their churches, fire departments, sources of income, and schools. Their entire community was in complete chaos. Imagine if during the biggest crisis in your life your entire support system was unavailable. That's exactly what happens in a disaster—life is completely suspended in time.

Rural communities are the backbone of not only our state but the country. They grow amazing produce, run small businesses, and take care of their neighbors. I have watched these communities over the years, some of them multiple times, lose their infrastructure and buildings, but they haven't lost their sense of community. No matter how high the water rises, the communities always seem to rise higher. I knew that in the days and months to come, Betty and her family, along with so many more, would begin to rebuild their lives yet again. Federal and state disaster programs are helpful, but it will take years for people to receive funding, and these funds are not enough to make people whole again. Thank God for the spirit of community.

In the blur of her stay at the shelter, I know that Betty will probably never remember me, but I will never forget her and what she taught me about resiliency. Yes, Betty, I do believe that God speaks to you, because I know I heard Him loud and clear through you. Thank you, Betty. The flood waters eventually receded. The Weather Channel, as well as most other media outlets, were long packed up and moved on to the next flash in the pan story. My heart was sad for all the people impacted, but this was a short blip and I needed to return to a full caseload at the practice and was preparing to take anatomy class in the spring for my RN pursuit.

Very soon after my shelter work, I was approached by my former employer asking me to run another CCP program post-Florence. As much as I loved the program and wanted to say yes, it was a temporary job, and I couldn't endure another season of unemployment hell. Instead, I offered to serve part-time as a consultant. Quickly, due to the dire impact and need for behavioral health support, I became full-time again with disaster recovery.

This time, though, I was so fearful of being unemployed after that I continued to see a caseload of almost twenty hours per week.

In March of 2019, I was full-time with a staff of eighteen counselors covering five counties. Generally, this grant terminates around the one-year anniversary of the event. Working on this timeline, my husband and I made plans that I would begin to phase out my clients and finish this grant in preparation for RN school. So here I was again, about to jump out of a perfectly good airplane. Winding down my practice … yes, again … and ending HOPE 4 NC grant … yes, again. I would be full-time in prerequisite classes for RN school and working on my deaconess classes along the way, which had been sidelined during my Florence recovery work. After months of powering through sixty-plus hours a week, it seemed that all disasters were safely under control and a good plan was in place. As a disaster recovery expert, I should have been leerier. It was the proverbial calm before the storm.

Survival

Shock and Denial

"Do not judge me by my successes, judge me by how many times I fell down and got back up again."

—Nelson Mandela.

IN THE EARLY 1960S, a book called *On Death and Dying* was authored by psychiatrist Elizabeth Kubler-Ross. This book is the primer for any grief counselor in training. In her work, she outlines what she had observed as the five stages of grief. Initially these were denial, anger, bargaining, depression, and acceptance. Over the years, other models have been expounded to broaden this work.

No two people, even experiencing an identical traumatic event, will go through grief the same way. I tell all my clients in their initial session that grief is like a thumbprint. Each person has a unique pattern of how they will grieve. With my therapy kids, we stamp our fingerprints on paper and make flowers, caterpillars, and all kinds of crazy creatures to see how unique each pattern can be. We also won't go through the stages in a neat and tidy package. Oh no, it's going to be a great big mess.

The first stage is shock. People in shock can react in ways that are bizarre or seem silly to others. In second grade during a school tornado drill, I broke my nose. Yes, an odd but true story. I remember being so upset because my mom had just polished my saddle oxford shoes, and they were now covered in bright red blood. Tears streaming and blood pouring, I insisted to my teacher that my mom was going to be so mad at me. My precious teacher assured me that my injury would get me not only newly polished shoes but likely all the treats I wanted as well. Boy, was she ever right!

August in Eastern North Carolina means brutal heat. These are the kind of late summer days where the humming cicadas cry out for a hint of a fall breeze. It was now August 2019, almost a year since Hurricane Florence made landfall. My team of crisis counselors, including myself, were starting to feel the compassion fatigue. The days were long and filled with heaviness and much frustration as we advocated for survivors to get the support they still desperately needed. Disaster recovery work is fraught with potential for compassion fatigue, and our passion that initially drew us to the work was beginning to fade. I was also still seeing clients in private practice and juggling activities for three teenagers. Yes, always the sadist.

I decided that I needed to take a weekend for self-care before the craziness of back-to-school hit for my kids and now myself again. With the hectic pace of life, it had been a few years since I'd had the time to take a trip back home to Elkin. My emotional bank account was way overdrawn, and I was hopeful that a trip to my roots would be the reboot my soul needed. There was no way I could have anticipated how important this trip would be to ground me before the biggest quake of my life.

Driving into town, so much nostalgia hit me: memories of trips to Royal's downtown soda shop with my mom for a cherry smash soda followed by hours spent in the public library choosing the perfect books. While many things looked the same, there were many noticeable changes in my hometown. This area, which used to be known for textile mills and tobacco farms, was now a happening tourist destination full of wineries and outdoor hiking trails. A genius economic move to simulate these communities, yet ironic since many of these counties were dry counties not that long ago, selling no alcohol at all.

This was my first trip home since publishing *Elizabeth and Stella Meet ZOE*, so I stopped by to donate a copy to the local library. As a little girl, I secretly dreamed that my name would one day be on a book in a library, but I never really thought that would happen. Now, here I was holding that dream. I just imagined a little child pulling my book off the shelf and getting excited to take it home. Who knows, maybe he or she will become the next local author.

It was a beautiful day, and I noted as I walked around the absence of humidity I had left behind. That wasn't the only thing I'd left behind. I felt so free and relieved of so much pressure. I knew I needed this respite, but there's nothing like laying it all down to know how heavy your invisible backpack has become. I sat on the bench by the library and took in all the scenery. It just felt so good to let it all go and just be. The irony was not lost on me that this same scenery that now soothed my middle-aged soul was what I couldn't wait to see in my rearview mirror as a rebellious teenager. Funny how time changes your perception.

I arrived at my former church cemetery as the sun was making its journey behind the steeple. It was my favorite time of day to be in this place. The sun's rays split behind the steeple and cascaded an illumination over the cemetery. The warmth of the rays on my skin felt like the presence of Christ, and I felt safe.

In grief counseling, you find that there are two very distinct camps: cemetery and non-cemetery people. I'm a cemetery person. For me spiritually, even though I know they aren't there, I get a lot of peace and encouragement in this place. Walking the cemetery, I feel the harsh reality of just how quickly time passes. Reading stones of not only my family but influential people in my community and faith, I realize how long some of my family and church members have been gone. My father has now been dead for more years than I spent with him. These are the moments that shake me and make me question how I want to spend the rest of my life.

I sat on the grass near my family's stones. Oddly, I noticed the same car driving by slowly several times. I tried to focus on the otherwise stillness and soak in the peace. After several very slow drive-by passes with serious rubbernecking, the car finally pulled into the cemetery. The driver had a strong look of concern on her face, and I could see that she was on her phone. I could just hear the phone call now: "Hey, Betty, there's a foreigner in the cemetery. I'm going down to take a closer look."

I waved to her and said, "Come on down, we're having a family reunion." Hey, if I'm lucky, she brought a cake to share with us. She quickly backed out and left me to my peace. Either she had received confirmation that I was authorized to visit here, or she was headed to get reinforcements. Time will tell.

Reentering from my trip that Sunday, I recounted all my adventures with my husband of my time spent with friends and family. As I had hoped, my soul was refueled by hours of long laughs with my cradle baby friend, Misty, and lots of hugs and love with the Hincher family. It's so unsettling now to think that I had no idea what would be coming my way in a few short days. I've often wondered how much my husband sensed what was coming and how close he thought he was to the edge.

It's true that time and apparently tragedy waits for no one. Right in the middle of my to do list four short days later, my life was interrupted in a way I never saw coming. My thoughts raced between work tasks, kids starting school, and my own upcoming classes, which then led to questioning myself for the thousandth time about my decision to take on schoolwork again.

I stop what I am doing and sit down with the phone to listen to my husband.

Breathe ... just breathe, I tell myself.

My thoughts and heart are racing. My kids ... oh my God, I can't live if something happened to one of my kids.

I feel sick; I can sense the weight. There's a long pause, and part of me doesn't want him to speak at all because the moment he does, whatever has happened will be real. There will be no going back.

The words roll out.

"I was just fired from my job. I've been embezzling. It's a lot of money, and we're ruined."

I recognize my husband's voice, but the words don't seem to align. In this moment, I feel as if I'm floating outside my body and watching this happen to someone else. This was the same man who just served with me six weeks ago helping people who are struggling in adverse poverty in Guatemala. How can this be true?

Reflecting on those first seconds and minutes, I marvel at the power and gift of shock. These moments are where we see the true reason God designed the fight or flight response. This biological mechanism was hardwired to kick in because without it, we wouldn't be able to survive some of life's most difficult blows. The brain goes into what we call amygdala hijack. This means that our body is totally on autopilot, and we are wired to handle almost anything for a short period of time.

The downside of amygdala hijack is that our brain is locked out of connecting with our prefrontal cortex. This is the area of the brain responsible for logical thinking, problem solving, and decision making. This is also a protective feature of the brain. In many traumatic situations, if the brain could accurately process the full impacts of the event, the body would completely shut down and we would die.

As the word sank in, initially I felt a tinge of relief because no one was dead, especially my kids. Yes, this was bad, but if no one had died, there was still hope to redeem the situation. We can't bring back the dead, but most other things can be dealt with.

Before I had a chance to speak, he continued.

"I wanted to wait to tell you this when I got home, but I'm not coming home."

Whoa, wait. What did he just say?

He proceeds to tell me where the life insurance policies are filed. My brain begins a rapid scrambling of neuron fires that, if audible, probably sound like Houston talking to the space shuttle as it launches.

"Fight or flight brain shut down in 3 ... 2 ... 1. Deploy rational brain crisis counselor mode in 3 ... 2 ... 1."

Talking people out of their own crisis is a delicate skill, learned through advanced training and years of practice on how to stay calm. Talking people out of crisis when you yourself are in crisis is a street skill learned because you've been doing this since you were a kid.

Frogs and Princes

"So this is the miracle That I've been dreaming of mmmm, mmm ... So this is love."

—Cinderella

MY HUSBAND AND I met while we were in college at East Carolina University. My dad insisted that I had to live in the same apartment complex as my distant cousin, who was a male, or it was a no-go for me to attend. Well, not only did I wind up in the same building, but our apartments were also side by side, and his roommate was my future husband. Yes, I literally married the boy next door.

It wasn't love at first sight, because I don't believe in that or soulmates, just to be clear. We just enjoyed being together and had a lot of fun. While I'd also like to say that I don't believe in fairytales, the hard fact remains that I got married at Walt Disney World. Yes, it was pretty awesome, and no, we didn't ride in that insanely overpriced carriage. I've always been a huge Disney lover, but I never set out to get married at FantasyLand, USA.

Like most respectable Southern girls of my day, I was planning a church wedding at my home church. For those who haven't had the pleasure, planning a wedding can be very taxing, and truth be told, it can make you lose your religion. Add to that my family situation, which was complicated by a mentally ill mother who could offer no support, an estranged relationship with my sister, and a dad who was slowly losing his battle to colon cancer.

One day I was sitting on the floor of my apartment, which looked like a kindergarten cut and paste session on steroids. Magazine cut outs all over the floor everywhere. Glossy images of flowers, table decorations, hairstyles, and Lord knows what else swirled all around me. I just lost it. Complete meltdown city. While the planning was overwhelming, the constant nagging thought was if my dad would live long enough to walk me down the aisle. All these decisions seemed pointless and paled in the deep shadow of loss that loomed over me.

Wedding planning breakdown number twenty-four safely under control, I returned to my cut and paste session. There it was, the answer to all my stress, the advertisement for Disney's Fairytale Weddings. Bibbidi-bobbidi-boo, bring it on, Fairy Godmother! In 1997, destination weddings weren't as commonplace as today. Believe me, I endured some serious lip service from some family members regarding this decision, but it took a huge load off of me and my family during a most impossible time.

My husband and I spent twenty-seven years together, twenty-three of those married. Like most couples, we've shared our highs and lows along this journey together. We had a good balance of sharing the workload of running a house as well as co-parenting. My husband could cook, clean, do laundry, and take care of children just as well as I could. These were qualities that my dad had possessed, and I would have accepted no less in a life partner.

My husband was the romantic of the marriage. I am way too practical. He bought flowers and cards for no reason, and I always felt loved. He was also attentive to my emotional needs and was an incredible sense of support in my life. He was a champion of every pageant and dance pursuit as well as every higher education adventure I ever wanted to take on. He boarded planes with me to Kenya and Guatemala and rolled up his sleeves to volunteer alongside our family at so many events. He was the silent presence every night while I cried myself to sleep after my dad died and through the never-ending nightmare of my family's mental health struggles. To me, this was true love and what being married was all about—a partner to ride the waves of life with you.

Working as a marriage and family therapist definitely has pros and cons related to your personal life. I acquired a lot of knowledge of what works to help relationships thrive. We prioritized our relationship by having regular date nights and traveling away together several times per year without our kids. On the flip side, I also saw so much deviant behavior as a therapist that I likely minimized some of his behaviors that I should have taken more seriously early on.

When our youngest child was a few months old and the girls were toddlers, he took them to visit his parents on a Saturday to give me a break. Instead of taking a nap or watching a good chick flick, I did what all new moms do: ran myself ragged cleaning up the house. While cleaning in our office area, I noticed his briefcase, and it was like a little voice in my head kept saying, "Look inside; you need to look." I was like no, that's his private work stuff, and I have no business in there. But the feeling just increased.

I locked the bedroom door just in case I didn't hear two toddlers and a screaming infant enter the house. My heart was pounding already, as if in anticipation that something wasn't right. The briefcase had a lock code; lucky for me, he always used the same passwords, so it immediately clicked right open. Initially, all the contents seem valid: checkbook, household bills, but then there was a paper with an email account and password. Hmmm, at this time in our marriage, separate from our work email accounts, we only had one personal joint email account

My heart rate was increasing as I logged into the account. By now I wasn't believing in luck but rather divine intervention, because the password to this account was written right on the paper. I could feel the heat rise in my neck and face as I speculated on what I would find when that account loaded. As the internet became more and more used and accessible, we as counselors were inundated with marriage sessions that focused on pornography addiction, so I wasn't surprised to see subscriptions to porn sites. But what I was shocked to discover was an email soliciting the services of a call girl as well as online gambling.

So many emotions were going through me. Hurt, anger, disappointment, and confusion. However, when you've been the "fixer" and problem solver all your life, you don't deal in emotions, so my analytical brain took over. Instead of feeling all the things I should have allowed myself to feel, I went into crisis mode, which is my comfort zone when things in my life feel out of control. While I was angry, I didn't want to destroy my family, so how could this be fixed?

I quickly printed out the email he had sent, put things away, and left the house before they returned. A babysitter was coming that evening because we had made dinner plans. I called him and told him I was doing some work at my office and to meet me there before we went. I knew I needed to be in my place of power to make this confrontation.

I was very firm in my confrontation, and of course there were all the typical responses: "I never met her. It was just a conversation. I would never cheat on you. I haven't been in those accounts for months. It was one bad day." I told him that he had to agree to counseling and do all the things necessary to restore my trust. He willingly accepted the terms of the agreement.

It never occurred to me at this point to not fight for the marriage. I married for life, and I believe we are all fallible people. Everyone makes mistakes; we all have the propensity to get lost and sidetracked. I like to think I give people the grace and chances I hope to be given when I mess up. If the tables were turned, I'd hope that my husband would feel that our marriage and family were worth the fight.

No matter how much I believed I was doing the right thing, working through this was a hard season of our marriage ... a very hard season. I was postpartum, with leaky boobs and already feeling crappy about myself as a woman. Now my marriage was on the rocks, and I was competing with porn stars and call girls. I had already had to humble myself to my midwife for STD testing. I didn't feel I could be more humiliated. Then one day I was in Walmart, and out of nowhere, panic struck. He managed all our finances. What if he had gambled all our money away? I left my cart right in the middle of the aisle and headed to my car. I went to the nearest credit union and opened my own account. Until further notice, I would be keeping all my money separate.

We attended counseling sessions, and he seemed to be doing all the things he could to restore our marriage. He had an accountability partner to address his addictions and even decided to get baptized, because he had never made that commitment. It took years, but I eventually rebuilt my trust with him, even to the point of putting our finances back together. This experience in our marriage, though hard, had made us a better couple. Additionally, it made me more passionate about my work with other couples. I truly believed that hard times could not only be overcome but that you could create something stronger than before. I really thought that we had built something so beautiful out of brokenness. Now I know that we had just slathered a very thick coat of paint over decaying wood.

Anger/Bargaining

"Grief and resilience live together."

—Michelle Obama

I CAN'T EMPHASIZE ENOUGH that the stages of grief are not linear, and we don't go through them in a nice, orderly fashion. One also must be prepared to face and sit with some very uncomfortable emotions, and I do mean very uncomfortable. We struggle to feel these strong emotions; we aren't good at this at all. Things can also get rather complex when we're simultaneously feeling so many conflicting emotions, such as intense anger and love for the same individual.

Therapists don't encourage categorizing emotions as good or bad because we know that all emotions serve a purpose. We refer to difficult emotions as uncomfortable or unpleasant emotions. However, it's human nature to label things as good or bad, acceptable or unacceptable. We live in a society that has taught us to believe that any emotions that don't make us feel good or happy are bad and should be avoided at all costs. Consumerism relies on us seeking to soothe these uncomfortable feelings with new products, things, or experiences. We spend tons of money on entertainment, homes, cars, expensive vacations, substances, and other escape mechanisms to avoid facing our true thoughts and feelings.

Of all these emotions that we deem unacceptable, feeling angry gets a very bad rap. From a young age we're not only taught that anger is a negative emotion but often shamed about feeling anger, especially as a woman. As a counselor I know that feeling anger is a normal human emotion and that repressing that anger is a huge contributor to depression or other health issues. Cognitively I know this, but it will probably take me a lifetime to rewrite the negative childhood belief that anger is bad and you should quickly shut it down in yourself and others.

Most of us are frozen developmentally in preschool mode on how to properly express and work through angry feelings. Anger is simply the outward manifestation of much deeper issues, often related to hurt, rejection, disappointments, or fear. So instead of being taught how to properly express our hurt or fear, we're quickly told to get it under control. Additionally, the codependents or people pleasers never wants anyone to be angry with them, so they need to soothe the person, which often means not standing up for themselves.

In reflection, my anger came on very quickly. While still reeling in shock, I moved rapidly that August day into anger. As soon as I hung up the phone with my husband, I was out the door. I headed to my office to drop off the food to my team and deliver my meeting agenda. No one would care whether I did these tasks or not, but that's autopilot. My body needed time to catch up to what my brain had just learned: my husband was an embezzler, and I was in a serious crisis. The day I found out my dad died, I walked back into the dance studio and taught ballet classes for the rest of the night. Until you can make sense of something, you do what you know and carry on as planned.

As I drove the short route to my office, everything seemed to be moving in slow motion. While it probably wasn't safe for me to be driving in that state of mind, driving has always been a way for me to calm my mind. I don't know what it is about driving on a winding country road, maybe it's my NASCAR roots, but the therapist in me suspects that the sense of control of where you can go with the car has a bit to do with the calming effect. In essence, when I drive, I have taken command of my chaotic situation.

My mind moves from paralyzed to racing thoughts. I replay the conversation. I hear the words. None of it made sense. Every nerve in my body is tingling and I am struck by a kind of fear I have never known. My stomach feels like it is full of lead weights and I am struggling to breathe. I hear the words over and over: "We are ruined". How could he do this to our family? Why? What was he thinking? What will happen to him? Will I be guilty by association? Will we lose our house? Where will we live? What will happen to our kids? A wave of nausea forces me to pull over and get out of the car. My rational brain thinks I need to call someone; I can't face this alone. My mind goes through the list. Sadie Jane … no, she's at work, Lynn, no I can't bother her. I sit down in defeat.

Then another feeling rushes to the forefront, like a huge ocean wave knocking me on my face. There it was, the root of this quick surge of anger: betrayal. If grief is the deepest level of human sadness, betrayal is the deepest level of human anger. Even greater the sting when you have given your partner another chance and they have betrayed your trust yet again. No one likes to feel made a fool. Anger and adrenaline in full force, survival mode kicks in and Mama Bear is ready to fight for her cubs. I will make those friend calls later; this round is just for me. I get back in my car, head home, and let the winding roads lull my heartbeat into a normal rhythm.

Control

The Art of Being Conned

"Fool me once, shame on you. Fool me twice, shame on me. Fool me three times, shame on both of us."

—Stephen King

FROM THE MOMENT I pulled into the driveway, something was way off. Call it what you will—a sixth sense, gut feeling, Spidey sense, the Holy Spirit—whatever it was, it was strong. This was just like the sensation I'd had years earlier to look in that briefcase, and this felt way more sinister than him making a one-time mistake. Experience has taught me to go with your gut; even if you don't understand the push, follow the instinct.

We walk inside in silence. I look at my husband of twenty-two years and, for once, I have no idea who sits before me. Who is this man? The man I was married to yesterday would not have put us in this situation. Less than twenty-four hours ago, we went on a dinner date, and I felt intimately connected to this person. Now I have a slight feeling of discomfort; already my sense of safety has been unhinged. So unsettling that a lifetime of connection can begin to fray in less than twenty-four hours.

Up until this point, I have very little experience dealing with people who break the law. I'm not a forensically trained therapist and never had the desire to be. While I didn't know exactly what normal reactions after being fired and busted for a federal crime might look like, I still knew enough about human behavior to know that things were just not adding up. His actions, words, and body language weren't congruent to the situation. He was like a caged animal, and his behaviors put me on alert.

I am now in complete rational mode. There are no emotions, just the facts. I tell him every word that comes out of his mouth better be the truth because this marriage is on the line. If I find out after today that there is one small detail that has been left out, I am done. Thus begins the famous quote, "I'm an open book." As I sit listening to him try to explain his actions that spanned over ten years and over $500,000, my mind begins to zone out. My body is here but my mind elsewhere.

I am hyper focused on two things. My primary concern is my kids and what will happen to their lives. I'm thinking about how they will be crushed to learn that their hero is a thief. My mind races, doing mental math, which is more proof that fight or flight can give you ridiculous skills, because I have always used my fingers and toes. I begin to make all kinds of contingency plans on how I can pay for a mortgage and everything on my own. Last week I was worried about how to fund braces, cars, and college; now I just wanted to keep a roof over our heads.

Equally strong is the fear of having to let go of my dreams and calling. Even during this survival instinct, I'm already feeling resentment towards him. His selfish acts not only cost our children unnecessary harm, but my whole life will be derailed. After years of dedicating myself to my children, they were about to fly the nest. This next phase was supposed to be about me. I was just coming to a place of finding myself after years lost in mothering and mid-life career struggles. At this moment, I am so devastated to think about abandoning my call to medical missions. I've spent so many years on this journey, and now to have to let that go is unimaginable. My chest feels physical stabs as I think of never returning to work in Kenya or Guatemala, or all the places the Lord has yet to call me. And yes, the anger meter is rising, this time rooted in fear of loss.

Suddenly, he jumps up and wants to go tell his parents what has happened. Yet another strange behavior, as he wasn't close to his parents at all. We would often go weeks on end without seeing or hearing from them, even though they only lived twenty miles away. I have sat in my in-laws' living room many times, but this is brutal. Silent tears roll down my face; I am in complete shock and am wrestling in my mind the next steps.

I barely hear what he tells them, but whatever the story, he garners their sympathy and manages to get a blank check to pay for an attorney. At the time, this seems like a natural thing for him to ask and for parents to assist with. However, it would later be revealed that he had also taken from their retirement funds to cover his schemes over the years. So much for him being an open book; unbeknownst to us, the con games continued.

We ride home in complete silence. Every minute feels like an hour. I walk in the door and grab my keys. I'm about to break, and it's time to fall apart. I jump in my car and head to my friend Lynn's house. I'm about to sound the alarm and summon a meeting of the Magnolia tribe.

Magnolia Tribe

"Blessed be the God and Father of our Lord Jesus Christ, the Father of mercies and the God of all consolation, who consoles us in all our affliction, so that we may be able to console those who are in any affliction with the consolation with which we ourselves are consoled by God"

(2 Corinthians 1:3-4)

THOUGH THERE ARE SO many verses I find inspiring, this is my favorite verse. It's also the scripture that confirmed my calling as a counselor. The image of God pouring out His love during my pain so that I might transfer that love to others is to me the essence of life. The human body and spirit were magnificently created to withstand trials that seem unbearable, but we were not designed to bear them alone. This strength is created as we join in community together.

In mental health when people are in crisis, one of the greatest indicators of coming through the event is a strong support system. If one thing in my life has turned out to be all that I imagined it should be, it's the bond of true friendships. One of my all-time favorite movies is *Steel Magnolias*. Any Southern girl my age can likely quote the entire movie. The magnolia flower is also the perfect symbol for resilience. Although it may appear delicate, it symbolizes endurance derived from the incredible ability to adapt over centuries in many different climates.

For all of history, women have depended on each other. If we searched, we could likely find the lost excerpts from Genesis, which states, "Then because men couldn't handle it, God created other women to help Eve bear the load." Please don't write me hate mail; this is not man bashing. While support is vital for both women and men, women have a strong need to live in connection with other women. Sadly, as our Western society has evolved, the image of the strong, independent woman has negated the importance of this sisterhood.

This was highlighted for me so deeply in my work with support groups. After speaking at a women's event years ago, I was approached by a mother who had endured the heartbreaking pain of losing her infant daughter. She inquired if I had ever thought about or would consider running a group for mothers who suffered miscarriages or infant loss. Her experiences with other grief groups just didn't match her needs. As I listened to her pain, I thought, *How could I sit with women who have endured the worst pain imaginable?* I've never felt so ill equipped to do anything in my life, so I wished her luck in finding someone to lead such an important group. I probably looked like Jonah fleeing for Nineveh as quickly as possible to get to my car.

A few months later, I started working with a new client who had suffered multiple miscarriages. After a few sessions, she looked at me and said, "No offense, you're really nice and supportive, but I need to connect with someone who has been through what I have." She was exactly right. As God would have it, I still had contact with the original lady who'd approached me, and together we created a grief support group for these women called "Footprints."

It's human instinct to ease negative feelings for people when things happen that we can't understand or comprehend. We feel like we have "to do" something in order to assist or help. When my dad was sick with cancer, the outpouring of love and support was overwhelming: calls, cards, visits, abounding acts of love, and even cakes that were auctioned off for hundreds of dollars to offset mounting medical bills. Fast forward a few years later, in the same community, my sister and I bore the load with little support as our mother battled bipolar disorder for over ten years. The very same people just didn't know what "to do."

Some of the most difficult but beautiful moments occurred in connection with these women in that grief group. They taught me a lot about enduring unimaginable pain and what post traumatic growth looks like. Even with years under my belt as a therapist, when I started this group, I didn't know what to say or do. Often when we don't know what to say or do, we accidently do the most injurious thing—nothing. In our effort to encourage someone in distress, we underestimate the most powerful tool that we could deploy—the simple gift of human presence. "I don't know what to say, but I'm going to walk with you, and I will not leave you." This is a powerful statement. Often there's nothing anyone can do or fix; we just need to not feel alone.

There's nothing more tried and true than that friend you have laughed with until you can't breathe, and you have a collection of adventures that no one else will ever understand. Deeper is that connection when that same friend has held you and wiped your tears in the deepest hell of your life. The ones that threw your bridal showers, dreamed with you as you painted a nursery together, carpooled kids to and from, and held your hand while you said goodbye to your parents. To live in this connection is the essence of life.

Funerals are always sad to me, but not for the obvious reasons. As I sit and listen to the caring acts or multiple ways that a person's life has intersected with others, I always think how wonderful it would have been for that person to know how others felt while they were living. To know how the smallest acts, which you probably disregarded, impacted others. What an incredible gift.

If we allow it, one of the blessings of living through a crisis is being alive to witness the acts of love that people share. Though I would never wish to relive the pain, I received the most incredible gifts through this hell. I got to see, feel, and experience the depth of love that so many people have for me and my children.

I have lived my life as a giver, and it returned to me in ways that I could have never imagined in my wildest dreams. I've tried to live a life loving people, and some days I succeed more than others. Call me crazy, but I think that every human being should feel loved, accepted, and live into their God given capacity. I guess at the end of the day I just long for connection.

From a young age, I never met a stranger, and to this day will still spark a conversation with anyone. I was a child abductor's dream come true. I mean, seriously, I'm so lucky that my picture didn't wind up on the side of a milk carton as a missing child. Sure, Mister, I'll help you find your lost puppy.

I'm 100 percent comfortable as the giver. The receiver? Yeah, not so much. This season awakened and exposed me to a vulnerability I never knew existed in me. I'm not comfortable in the role of receiver. After all, you only had to go to church once to know "It's more blessed to give than receive." The humility was instant.

No matter what this struggle makes me question, I will never question the importance of protective factors. Within the definition of resiliency, a significant part of protective factors includes social connections and concrete support in times of need. It's not necessarily what we go through but who we have surrounded ourselves with that defines how we walk through the trials. I can assure you, I would not be alive without these deep resources. In honor of my favorite movie, I call my friend network, The Magnolia Tribe.

Lynn is a vital part of my tribe; we've been friends for over twenty years. We have the same wicked sense of humor as well as a pact that whichever one of us dies first, we will ensure there isn't an open casket at the funeral. We refuse to have people standing over us while we're dead, blessing our hearts and talking about how good we look. It's just wrong. I sank into a chair in her living room and proceeded to tell her the day's surreal events. For a moment, I was safe. She acknowledged my right to shock and anger, but she also gave me the most important gift: hope. "Right now, I want you to focus one day at a time, and I'm with you no matter whether you stay with him or not, but promise me one thing—you are going to nursing school. That is your calling, and I don't care if I have to drive your kids around or buy your books, you are not giving up on that because of his mistakes."

I immediately began to cry because, without me saying a word, she had validated what I was feeling deep down. My whole life had been about doing the right thing and putting others before myself and feeling selfish or guilty if I pursued my passions. The fact that someone still saw my dreams as valid and important during all this chaos was huge for me. In life, all it takes, whether you're five years old or one hundred years old, is for someone to believe in you and support you. The strength that we so often admire in others is the reflection of the love and support we have poured into others coming right back at us.

If you would like to be initiated into The Magnolia Tribe, here is the job description:

Answer every call.

Support her no matter what.

Pack boxes.

Unpack boxes.

Repack same boxes.

Unpack same boxes.

Clean her house.

Take her food.

Text her encouragement.

Give her permission to break.

Tell her she is a badass.

Push her when necessary.

Promise to come get her out of bed when she can't.

Answer every single call.

Send her flowers on anniversaries or hard dates.

Send gift cards.

Ship her coffee on a regular basis.

Leave her a self-care bag.

Sit with her.

Answer every call.

Be reliable transportation to cart around her kids.

Other duties as requested.

The Magnolia Tribe does not discriminate on the basis of race, color, religion, gender, age, national origin, disability, marital status, sexual orientation, and yes, we even allow Yankees.

The Aftermath

*"O my God, I cry by day, but you do not answer;
and by night, but find no rest"*

(Psalm 22:2)

IN THE EARLY DAYS after a traumatic event, my clients often share a similar experience. There's this moment when they first wake up and say, "Oh, thank God, what a terrible nightmare; things are OK." Almost as quickly as the thought processes, reality slaps them in the face and then the gut punch comes again. The nightmare was indeed reality.

That's exactly what happened to me on Friday morning after learning the news. For a moment I looked around my bedroom. Everything looked in place, but then I realized my life was anything but the same. The panic kicked in. I jumped out of bed and quickly got dressed. I had to get to the bank fast. Our paychecks dropped into our accounts that morning, and I just prayed all the way to the bank that our account hadn't been frozen. This was the only money I had to my name. There was nothing in savings, no retirement, and I had no parents to turn to for financial support.

The night before I had sat down with him to go over our finances, or should I say lack thereof. What we owed versus the lies he had told me over the years was mind blowing. After seventeen years of paying on a mortgage, we owed what we'd initially borrowed. Are you kidding me? I might as well have been driving down the road and throwing my mortgage payment along the highway for all those years.

The line of credit I used to start my business in 2011, which I was told was paid off, was still there. The weight of all this debt was heavy. It felt like I had a hundred-pound backpack strapped on me and then I was tossed into the ocean. My greatest core belief of financial failure had been activated, and I was in survival mode. Worse, I knew at that moment it would be up to me to claw my way out of it. I no longer had a partner.

I put my card into the ATM and entered my code. I kept waiting for the screen to flash "Access Denied," but thankfully the money was there, and I was able to make withdrawals. Next I had to open a new account. Even now I can still hear the swishing sound as I walk in and the click of the bank door closing behind me. As I sat in the manager's office, I became keenly aware that I was very uncomfortable being in a financial institution. I sat there and thought about how many times my husband had done exactly what this manger was doing for me, and now he was headed to prison. A sick feeling washed over me.

I hadn't opened my own account in over ten years. I was responsible for people's mental wellbeing, but I had never logged into a digital banking platform. Sitting there with two master's degrees, I felt so intimidated and overwhelmed. When the manager asked me how she could assist me, she got quite the story to tell her family that night. I suddenly vomited the last twenty-four hours to her, and she then felt burdened to share her ugly divorce story and how she had rebuilt her credit. I felt a bit like I was in a movie and her body had been commandeered by an angel.

By the afternoon, I was sitting on one side of a banquet-size table in a law firm. I heard an imaginary clock ticking in my head. Time felt like it was barely moving. We were now twenty-four hours into a nightmare that felt more like it had been going on for months. Walking into the office, I had given my husband the opportunity to meet privately with his attorneys. I told him there are two people that you never lie to: your attorney and your therapist. He opted for me to be in the room. Their questions came in true lawyer style—quick and with no emotional response to our answers.

Did your kids have expensive hobbies? No.
Do you have a second home? No.
Do you have a boat or expensive cars? No.
Mrs. Harrell, did you have any knowledge of any of this? No.
The questions continued with a string of robotic answers: No, no, no.

When they finished, I was ready for my turn. My mind had been racing with fears and questions that I needed answered. I wanted to know what my liability was and could they take our home. They reassured me that most likely with him being forthcoming we would know about any actions moving forward. While I still felt unsettled, I walked out feeling some sense of relief.

Less than three weeks later, I turned down my street to find my home looking like a CSI crime scene. Agents searched my entire home top to bottom. Every kid's room, underwear drawers, and attic contents. If I had one shred of dignity left, this ripped it completely away. I had never felt so helpless, violated, and exposed in my life. As I walked with the agent to unlock the cars for him to search, he said to me, "This isn't what we were expecting to find; there's nothing here to show for all this missing money. Does he have another family somewhere?" To which I replied, "I don't know, but if he has another wife, she should freaking come and get him."

Fight, Flight, Freeze

"Every experience God gives us, every person He puts in our lives is the perfect preparation for the future that only He can see."

—Corrie Ten Boom.

THE NEXT FEW WEEKS were a blur of events. My days were packed with work and meetings with attorneys, accountants, therapists, and pastors. There was a never-ending list of tasks that had to be handled now that I was solely responsible for the wellbeing of our children. I had to simultaneously work and handle all these fires because the bills continued to roll in. Every step was executed with a completely mind-numbing automation. Again, thank God for the fight or flight response, because to this day I have no idea how I did it all. I was still managing a team of eighteen crisis counselors and seeing patients in the clinic. Everywhere I went I felt like people could see straight through me like a transparent sheet of paper.

One thing I've always prided myself on as a counselor is healthy boundaries with my clients. Practicing in rural areas is a little more challenging because people tend to know everyone. There's nothing like driving through the local Sonic to get your late-night milkshake and have a teenager say, "Yo, this is my counselor. Ya'll come say hey!" One day not too long after D Day, I met with a long-standing client of mine. I had worked with this client and his family on and off for fifteen years through all kinds of life issues. I started the session, and I thought I was doing a great job of pressing through. I was caught off guard when he leaned forward and said, "Melissa, is something wrong? You don't seem like yourself." I immediately broke into tears and gushed out a four-sentence version of the recent events. He sat back and said, "Sometimes people do stupid things, but you know, like me, maybe he will learn." This client had spent time in prison early in his life. We went back to his session and never spoke of it again.

I was always checking myself with colleagues to make sure I was safe for my clients. While therapists are empathic, good for me that our skills largely depend on the analytical parts of our brain. Amazingly, I still felt hopeful for my clients, just not for myself. When I would say to the new client with depression that things will get better, I believed it and meant it. I can remember taking a walk around my office one day and thinking, this is it, you just must learn to be content with existing. Everything good is over. It felt like death.

My kids weighed on my mind constantly. I believe in being as honest with kids as developmentally appropriate. Given all my knowledge of the impacts of trauma on kids, I was already worried about the immediate and long-term effects all of this would have on them. Together, my husband and I had fought so hard to give these kids the best start in life, and they literally went from an ACEs score of zero to four overnight. All of my mom life, I had stressed about all of the ways not to ruin my kids. I had ensured they learned compassion, drank organic milk, and didn't impale themselves with foreign objects. But I never thought I'd have to protect them from the actions of their own father. I was livid with him. How could he undo all of this good with such stupid actions? It just seemed so preventable and unnecessary.

I consulted my closest kid therapy friends as well as spiritual pastors, and we all agreed that walking this story out in bite-size pieces would be best. One of the best nuggets of advice came from one of my personal local superheroes, Tracey. I admire this lady's tender yet tenacious spirit. She has raised three boys, achieved a doctorate degree, and can still drive a tractor. These are my people! She reminded me that in the days following JFK's assassination, the country looked to Jacqueline Kennedy. If she had fallen apart, our whole national history might be different. "Your kids will follow your tone and lead, just like the country followed Jacqueline."

Initially we sat them down and told them that Dad lost his job, and it was his fault, and that was all we could share at this time. They would be taken care of, and we would keep them safe. As their dad's mental stability unraveled, I finally was faced with no choice but to tell them the truth … well, as much as I knew. I didn't want them to have a memory of this conversation associated with somewhere they loved, like our home. We were heading to Western North Carolina for the weekend to visit my sister, so I decided to stop at a Sheets convenience store along the way. I figured hey, if they never want to go there again, there are plenty of other options along the way. I handed them cash and told them to go in and get whatever drinks and snacks they wanted. This should have clued them in that something was about to go down, as that rarely occurred with this junk food police officer on duty.

We sat down outside, and I took in the three innocent faces of my children one more time. After this moment, they would forever be changed and would start to become wise beyond their years. They were about to cross the invisible line, and I was the bearer of the life-changing news. Watching their reactions to the news that their father had committed a crime and would likely go to prison will always be a moment that I wish didn't have to exist in our history together. I deal with trauma every single day, but when it's your own children, it's the most helpless feeling in the world. All I knew to do was just sit with them in the heaviness while they cried. Once again, there was nothing to do but just sit in the awfulness of it all.

I knew this was so much loss to take in at once. To go literally overnight from an intact, stable home with financial stability and positive parents to parental job loss, parents separated, and impending prison sentence of a parent ... I can't imagine trying to process all that at that age. I was in crisis trying to process it all as an adult with significant coping skills and support. After the tears had slowed and all the questions that could be answered that day were, we headed back to the car to resume the trip. My son looked at me and said, "Thanks, Mom."

"For what?"

"I will never ever want to go to a Sheets again." We both smiled and laughed. In that simple exchange, so much was communicated without the need for words. In that moment, I knew as hard as each step would be, the trauma bond was formed, and together we would make it one step at a time. My children were hurting and broken, but we were not destroyed.

Where Does My Help Come From?

"I lift up my eyes to the hills—
from where will my help come?
My help comes from the Lord,
who made heaven and earth"

(Psalm 121: 1–2)

THE NIGHTS WERE BRUTAL. While the days were long and hard, they were also filled with work distractions and seeing clients at night. You'd think after checking in with my kids I would fall into a hound dog drooling sleep. Not at all. That was when reality would hit me the hardest. The reality that I was alone. While I had a wonderful support system, I had lost my partner. In the day I was able to hide behind the brave and strong career woman armor that protected me from the crushing reality that I felt so utterly lost and alone. I was about to be the two things I never hoped I would be: divorced and a single mom.

I sat in my room alone and watched the shadows cast from the candle dance on my walls. Shadows brought two extreme emotions as a child: joy or fear. It was such an exhilarating feeling to try to catch my shadow and have it follow me around as I played outside. In the light of day, my shadow was a companion and friend, and everything around the shadow could be seen. But as night crept in and shadows blended into darkness, my shadow became less familiar and comforting and awakened a sense of fear of the unknown. This is how life comes at us. One minute we're basking in the glorious rays of sunlight, and everything seems possible. The next thing we know, a dark cloud descends upon us, and we are enveloped in a sense of doom.

I sat in my room on the floor, legs crossed, glass of wine in my hand, and the remainder of the bottle positioned within reach. How could I survive this? Every day was so hard. Tears flowed nonstop, my heart absolutely pounding out of my chest. The racing thoughts rushed in my mind like tidal waves: *What if I can't keep our home? Where will we live? Even if I work seven days a week, how can I ever get out of this deep hole of debt? Oh God, my kids! They're going to be so broken. They never asked for this.*

I got up from the floor, placed my glass down, and began to pray and invoke the name of Jesus over my entire house. As I have shared, I have belonged to many denominations along my faith journey, but never Pentecostal Holiness. On this night, at least for a few minutes, I was a convert. Whatever it took to save my kids from the fall out of this nightmare. I hovered outside the doors of each of my children and literally begged for the mercy of God on their safety and lives. "Lord, I don't care what happens to me anymore, but protect these innocent souls from all this damage."

One of the worst parts of going through this was the constant mind battle of what was real and what wasn't in my life. I began to look at all the family photographs. I once looked at these and felt such joy, with wonderful memories of times shared at the beach, Disney, or holidays. Now every memory I have feels tainted. Like every trip was paid for with "dirty" money. To stand around and look at pictures on the wall and wonder if it was reality, and what kind of dimension we were in. To look at pictures of my beautiful family and wonder if it was truth or a lie, and what really happened in all those moments. It's a surreal feeling that you'll never be able to explain unless you've experienced it. To step back and feel like you have enjoyed all this amazing connection and time woven into this fabric of your family and then to just wonder if it ever really existed.

It all rushed at me, full force—the reality that my life had forever been altered. That my husband would not come home, we would not go to dinner again and share a deep conversation. The fact that I had lost my best friend and the person I thought was my greatest supporter and helpmate, besides God. How I longed to fall into the arms of my parents and have someone take some of the load. For just one day, someone to take care of me, someone to say, "I've got this; now go rest." Those were the realities that faced me at midnight, at 1:00 a.m., at 2:00 a.m., until I eventually drifted off to sleep. Then I'd get up and do it all again.

Waking Up to Abuse

"One's dignity may be assaulted, vandalized and cruelly mocked, but it can never be taken away unless surrendered."

—Michael J Fox

COUNSELING WOMEN IN ABUSIVE relationships has always been a struggle for me. I really have to screen myself from saying, "Girl ... run ... he's a loser ... value yourself." No matter how many times I read the abuse cycle or knew the psychology, I was still so upset when my clients would go back. I pride myself on not being gullible. I don't fall for infomercials and fads. I truly believe if it seems too good to be true, it probably is. Sadly, I'm more of a pessimist hiding behind the mask of a hopeful human. So now here I was, in the ultimate plot twist of my life, a front row perspective I never wanted to see. Not only is this my partner of twenty-seven years, but I'm a skilled therapist who has been charmed, scammed, and left to fend for three kids. What did I miss? Am I just this stupid? How did I ever pass abnormal psychology?

Sure, there were issues years ago in our marriage, but I thought we'd worked through those. Any other behaviors that may have raised flags along the way were quickly put to ease by his now very apparent con skills. It was like driving on a two-hundred-mile road trip, and every fifty miles or so seeing a small brush fire. Then when you arrive at your destination, you realize that it was really one massive fire. What had seemed like his little personal struggles along the way was concealing a huge, blazing wildfire of a possible personality disorder.

When most people hear the term personality disorder, thanks to Hollywood, they think of multiple or split personalities. Those are extremely rare, but there are other personality disorders listed in the *Diagnostic and Statistical Manual of Mental Disorders* (*DSM-5*), which is our handbook for mental health diagnosis. While the causes of these are still difficult to pin down, a combination of genetic and environmental factors are the most suspected culprits.

Personality disorders usually bud and become evident during late adolescence or early adulthood. Traits and symptoms vary depending on the type of disorder. While these maladaptive traits can cause significant distress in people with personality disorders, they are very damaging to those around them. Unlike most individuals who seek counseling, people with personality disorders usually wind up in a therapist's office not because they're seeking help but due to the distress their disorder causes on others.

At twenty years old when I met my husband, I had no idea that I was a dream come true for someone with possible antisocial personality disorder (ASPD). People with ASPD are naturally drawn to those who are open, loving, and have a huge capacity for compassion and forgiveness. I've always had a deep capacity for empathy. In this era of psychology, I definitely fit the description of an "empath."

Up until sixth grade, I had never been in trouble at school besides for talking excessively in class, and I like to think that I transferred that demerit into a noble career. My mother was shocked one day to get a call that she had to pick me up from school because I'd been in a physical altercation with a girl in my class. I had watched this girl make fun of a boy in our class that day who had learning disabilities, and I was fired up. On our way down the hall for bathroom break, I told her what I thought, and it went south from there. While my mom was certainly not happy with my actions, she did support my advocacy. Hey, where do you think I learned all that empathy?

What I also didn't realize at age twenty was the damage that had been done to me growing up in all the dysfunction. I exhibited quite a few codependent traits spilling over from my childhood. Here are a few of my top traits:

- An exaggerated sense of responsibility for the actions of others
- A tendency to do more than my share, all the time
- A tendency to become hurt when people don't recognize my efforts
- An extreme need for approval and recognition
- A sense of guilt when asserting myself

It was so much just dealing with all the fallout of his behaviors, but to begin to process all of this was a staggering task. I was constantly analyzing and peeling apart the layers. It was mind blowing to see a person who I thought so selfless and moral have no capacity for guilt or remorse regarding his actions. Not only for the people he stole from but for the distress he had put his wife and children in. Who knew the greatest psychology case study of my life would be my own husband?

People with ASPD are master manipulators and pathological liars. Their motto in life is basically if it feels good and you can avoid the consequences, go for it. They love the high of getting away with things and feeling superior to others. If people with ASPD ever get exposed, often people are shocked that these are the qualities of this person, even close family members. Hence the term "the sociopath next door." I struggled with trying to wrap my mind around the possibility that I'd missed a personality disorder all those years. Believe me, in my line of work I'd been a few rounds with a narcissist or two, and I can usually spot them a mile away. However, covert narcissism is a very special animal. These people are loved and highly regarded by many, and all the while they can fool others that they are selfless, honest, and empathetic.

People with ASPD will often use a person as their cover, which gives them credence and legitimacy with others. This cover allows them to run their cons under the radar of those around them, even the closest ones. This definition seems to fit exactly what my husband did. I mean, who would think that the head church usher and local soccer coach with a good family was embezzling by day?

Once the mask was off, his behaviors were unbelievable. To keep our children in the only home they'd known, a few sets of friends offered to buy our home and I would rent it from them. He agreed that he would only sign to sell if he was allowed to live there. When asked to come and help sort through all the items in our attic before selling the home, his smug response was, "Let the bank take care of it. Not my problem." In his world, if there was nothing in it for him, then he wasn't showing up. The personality traits continue to match up.

Abuse takes many forms and shapes, and I think it's human nature to assign levels of severity to abuse. If you can see the signs from battery or from sexual assault, then it really happened. With emotional and financial abuse, people's opinions become very subjective. There's a fallacy that emotional abuse really isn't as bad because you don't have visible injuries, and with financial abuse the survivor should have known. This mentality also permeates the brain of the victims of emotional abuse. Even though I was a therapist, at this point I was a victim and unable to see the impacts of years of abuse. This vulnerability enables the gaslighter to do their thing. Gaslighting is a tool used by people with personality disorders, and it's so exhausting. Gaslighting makes you question reality. If I asked, "What did you do with all the money?" his response was, "I took it to live, basic things like groceries, etc." Then I would think, *Well, maybe that's true and I just never knew.*

I already questioned myself about so many things, but he was making me feel like I was crazy. He constantly presented a false narrative, which led to more confusion on my part. In my head, I could hear myself constantly questioning. *Maybe I did do that, or maybe I caused that to happen.* Or he would prey on my deep core beliefs: "You're a good Christian woman, so I know you can forgive me and we can get through this." While I had overcome most of my need to please people over the years, the thought of disappointing God was still a huge fear, and there the likely personality disorder had me, and he knew it.

Refined by Fire

"In this you rejoice, even if now for a little while you have had to suffer various trials, so that the genuineness of your faith—being more precious than gold that, though perishable, is tested by fire— may be found to result in praise and glory and honor when Jesus Christ is revealed"

(1 Peter 1:6–7)

I'VE ALWAYS EXPECTED MY faith to be tested. I was never taught, nor do I believe, that by following Jesus I am assured financial blessing and physical wellbeing. In fact, I'm more inclined to believe that if you're trying to follow Jesus, you had better suit up for the fight of your life. I am nauseated by the entire concept of prosperity religion. It's counterintuitive to my understanding of what it means to be a disciple of Christ. Many of the most spiritually rich people I've ever met were, by global standards, the poorest of the poor.

Just like any relationship, our spiritual quest is fraught with various seasons and trials. In some seasons I have felt so close to God in worship that it was as if I had touched the very hem of His garment. Other times I've felt like I had been sold the emptiest promise ever. "Like seriously, this is it?" I could relate to Job's wife and wonder if it was time to curse God and die.

I never thought losing my marriage would be the ultimate test of my faith. I'm not a trained street fighter, but if you look so hard for the blow to come from one direction, you'll likely get gut punched when you aren't looking. No, I expected the greatest test of my faith would occur abroad on the mission field, in some type of dramatic life or death moment.

When you're working on the mission field and faced with dangerous situations, being labeled a Christian can be a good title. Kind of like a free pass of safety. However, other times any sign of Christianity is literally a target on your back. Many people are surprised to learn that Kenya is largely a Christian nation. This is counter to their neighboring country, Somalia, who barely has enough Christians to register on the scale. Much conflict occurs at the border of these two vastly different nations.

On one trip, our driver stopped and said he didn't feel safe taking us any further due to the danger of conflict in the region. You could feel the entire mood of the team shift. Panic struck, and I looked around. People were frantically removing any symbols that would identify them as a Christian. I remember thinking to myself, *This is it ... here it is the ultimate test. If you get a knife to your throat and are asked do you believe in Christ, what will you say?* Would I be Peter and deny Him in order to live? Or would I be Stephen and confess to my death?

Thankfully, up until this point I haven't had to get the answer to that question. My heart wants to believe I would stand strong, but the biologist in me bets that the amygdala would win, and I would deny God. Remember, the brain is built to survive. This current test of my faith didn't present as a thirty-second choice to live or die; it was a long-drawn-out process of wrestling with what it means to truly forgive another human being.

There was no way around forgiveness; my faith requires it. Our entire doctrine is built around forgiveness. I know that I can't be reconciled to God if I harbor unforgiveness of another person in my heart. How can I ask for forgiveness from God when I'm not able to bestow it on others? The act of forgiveness was not what caused my distress, because I've seen what bitterness does to a person in my work and within my family. I knew that beyond my faith, forgiveness would be necessary for me to ever have freedom of my heart to move on again.

No, the push and pull came while struggling with reconciliation. In a marriage, once you forgive, you begin reconciliation. Within the first twenty-four hours after the events went down, there was no doubt in my mind that this marriage was over. I even wrote in my journal only two days after I learned of his crimes:

> *"I know I should want to fix this, but how many times do I have to sacrifice and be betrayed? While I do not wish to break my children, I am done with this marriage."*

But after forgiveness and reconciliation once in this marriage, the mental health professional knew the odds of his behavior changing were not high. I had to accept that my husband had a serious issue beyond one mistake, and I had to look out for my mental health and that of my children.

Sitting in our pastor's office and telling my husband that I wanted a separation was something I never imagined would happen. Just because your head knows something is the right choice doesn't mean your heart does. It truly would have been easier to stay with him. One would think that given the gravity of the situation we were in, my husband would understand and acquiesce to whatever his wife needed. No, the tables were turned, and true to the likely personality disordered brain, he embraced his role of victim. "How could you abandon me in my time of need?" he asked me, as I stood knee-deep in the mess he had created. It was never about the impact of his actions on anyone else; it was about what he was losing or suffering. Never about me, his children, or those he stole from.

I desire to live in peace with others, but especially those I am close to. If I've done something to offend you, I want to know and set it right. This desire to live in peace, while mostly a good thing, can also guilt those of us with certain personalities into allowing people to take advantage of us. Setting up boundaries with someone with a personality disorder is very difficult. It's a lot like dealing with a two-year-old who wants a cookie before dinner. You do well for the first bit of time, and finally they wear you down and you say, "Here, just take the dang cookie!"

I visited with an attorney to file separation papers and begin the divorce process. As if the emotional pain of all this wasn't enough, I was disgusted to find out that the law viewed his criminal behaviors separate from our marriage issues. Basically, me filing for separation and divorce was no different than if I had woken up that day and said, "Yeah, I'm all done with this. I want a divorce." He was still entitled to everything 50/50, and because I was working, technically I could owe him alimony. Yes, people, crime does apparently pay.

When bad things happen or we struggle, the church and our church family should be the number one place we can go for comfort, support, and understanding. That's true for certain events such as death, illness, or other tragedies. In these moments, we embrace our church family, and for me and my children, we did find love, support, and shelter there. I was very fortunate to have pastors and other faith mentors along my journey who were educated on abuse and mental illness. Sadly, many are given misinformation and traumatized further by clergy or church members who guilt them into staying in abusive marriages with twisted religious ideas.

Probably my strongest saving grace along the way was the incredible cautions that would be presented to me through actual physical sensations or things put before me. In my faith, we call it the Holy Spirit. These things would miraculously happen at times when I was questioning deeply my choices regarding believing him or entertaining the idea of restoring the marriage. One of the most spiritual experiences happened in a prayer garden near my house. I went there after a difficult counseling session in which we had gone round and round about him moving out and boundaries. I'd been to this garden a few times to journal and pray over the years. I closed my eyes and just allowed my mind to release all thoughts and be open to what God had to say to me. Suddenly, I saw an image of my husband and I walking and holding hands; we looked at each other, smiled, and then released hands and walked separate ways until I could no longer see either of us. I can feel the goosebumps even now as I recall that vision. I opened my eyes, and in that moment, I felt free and that God had released me from my marriage.

Holiday Hell

*"Every Who down in Who-ville, the tall and the small,
Was singing! Without any presents at all!
He HADN'T stopped Christmas from coming!
IT CAME!
Somehow or other, it came just the same!"*

—Dr. Suess, *The Grinch Who Stole Christmas*

BOTH OF MY PARENTS died in December, so as all the Christmas decor goes up, so does my level of anxiety and depression. Through my intense losses, just as the Grinch discovered, like it or not, no matter how we might stop it from coming, life goes on, and the holidays do not wait for us to have our life in order. In 2008, celebrating Christmas morning with our three small children running about with Christmas PJs on and reindeer antlers atop their heads was most definitely the last thing I wanted to be doing that day. I was still in shock from my mom's sudden death and had just attended her funeral only two days prior.

As grueling as that experience had been, this year was simply unbearable. Could I just go to sleep and pretend Christmas never happened? Tear the month off the calendar and pretend it was January? My kids still give me a hard time about how we moved all the clocks up in the house for New Year's Eve when they were young so they thought they got to stay up until midnight. Yep, I'm pretty sure at this age they would figure out if I literally skipped an entire month.

I tried to keep things as normal as possible for the kids, keeping as many of our traditions intact as possible. Not one part of my being wanted to drag out the Christmas tree, but I figured it was just one more task to power through. One more first to get through and check off the list. I envisioned that with enough holiday tunes, hot chocolate, and cookies, we could temporarily divert the pain and find some tiny pieces of joy. What I forgot in this hot chocolate induced euphoria was that our Christmas tree was like a living history of our family. As soon as I opened the boxes and began removing the decorations, I immediately regretted this decision. Like so many other families, every ornament tells a part of our family journey: our first married Christmas, baby's first Christmas, the piles of handmade school projects, and a commemorative ornament from every trip we had ever taken as a family. The sense of loss and wrongness was so heavy, but there was no going back now.

I began to think to myself that there should probably be a special memory service for divorces, similar to funerals. I know … a morbid thought, but divorce is the death of a family, and so much of it goes unrecognized. Many well-meaning people will say, "Oh, that's bad, but you'll find someone better." Even if better days are ahead, there are still good things that should be remembered and honored. Those good memories are what tether you and make it so difficult to move on.

On Christmas Eve, my husband came to stay the night to be with the kids. In the past we had a very set routine on Christmas Eve. We all attended church and had dinner, and then my husband and I stayed up late into the night sharing time and exchanging our gifts. To avoid possible engagement with him and to distract myself from the complete awfulness of pain, I attended three church services. I worshipped with the Baptists, Methodists, and Catholics. You know, I must keep that faith passport up to date! I also solved a long mystery I had wondered about for years. If you want to know who hangs out at the local convenience store on Christmas Eve, apparently it's people trying to avoid dealing with family members they don't want to see. I can assure you, it's not for the food.

With all the new demands and extra work hours, I had put a pause on pursuing my nursing classes. Feeling this incredible sense of loss of working towards my goal, one day I decided to Google "Training classes for medical missionaries" in hopes of at least finding an online course. Well, what do you know, I found a two-week intensive course designed to equip you with the knowledge and hands-on experience you need to diagnose and treat illness and injury in remote locations. This would be perfect, but I was sure that it would be far away or ridiculously expensive. I couldn't believe it when I found out that it was here in North Carolina, and they also offered me a scholarship. One holiday miracle found in the middle of otherwise unending distress and pain.

From Practice to Pandemic

> "This is the way the world ends
> Not with a bang but a whimper."
>
> —T.S. Eliot, "The Hollow Men"

AS MUCH AS I love Western North Carolina, I do not love winter at all, which is one main reason I left. Even with milder winters here down east, I still loathe January and February. It was helpful to have the Medical Mission Intensive (MMI) offered through Equip International (equipinternational.org) to look forward to in March to get me through these months. I distracted myself for hours poring through the preparatory materials. I was thrilled to be back in global health textbooks learning about malaria, tuberculosis, measles, Ebola, and other tropical diseases. Yes, a sickness, I know.

As March rolled around, there were so many things that I was looking forward to at MMI, or "jungle nurse school," as my mission friend renamed it. There was the excitement of getting to learn all these incredible skills, and I was so looking forward to getting away and removing myself from all the stress. What I didn't anticipate was what would happen when all the plates stopped spinning and I had time alone with my thoughts and emotions that had been brewing and building for months shoved back into the deepest recoil of my soul.

The triggers started almost immediately, even as I began driving west. Flashbacks of so many trips with my husband back home for visits and vacations. Walking into the grocery store in a small Western North Carolina mountain town was something my husband and I had done on many trips. I quickly grabbed what I needed and got out. The sounds of hotel doors sliding open and closing made me cringe. I had rarely been in a hotel without him since we got married.

We started each day with a short chapel service. Sitting in the small chapel each morning as we had devotions before class began awakening all my grief of those gone. When you're in a PTSD crisis, all your wounds are open and fair game. Despite battling my PTSD symptoms, my spirit was full, which deepened my calling into missions. Prior to going to MMI, I had completed an interview with our local Community Action Organization and was offered a new grant position to serve as the Mental Health Coordinator for Head Start/Early Head Start. Once I returned home, I would be wrapping up crisis disaster work and starting my new job. While my horse was still very much off the path I had planned, MMI and starting this new job felt like the directions I had seen myself on before.

My time at MMI exceeded my expectations, but when they say intensive, they mean it. For two weeks we were immersed in hands-on classes all day and spent late into the evenings working on case studies. During the two weeks we were there, I watched no TV and read no news; we were in our own bubble. By the time we completed our course on March 20, 2020, North Carolina was about to go on lockdown due to the COVID-19 pandemic. While we had been studying all kinds of infectious diseases that were mostly eradicated due to vaccinations here in the US, COVID-19 had taken over the nation like wildfire.

Driving home from Western to Eastern North Carolina that day was one of the most eerie feelings of my life. It felt like the beginning of the apocalypse. There were hardly any cars out, and trying to navigate bathroom and gas stops with so many things closed was very unsettling. Having not been home for over two weeks, my house needed serious supplies for three hungry teens. I managed to find one store that was open, ran in like a fire drill, grabbed what I could, and ran out. As I finished the drive home, I thought to myself, *Seriously Lord, what is next?* Considering my experiences of the past few years, I immediately retracted that statement because I was afraid of what the answer might be.

One Brave Koi Fish

"Therefore, since we are surrounded by so great a cloud of witnesses, let us also lay aside every weight and the sin that clings so closely, and let us run with perseverance the race that is set before us"

(Hebrews 12:1)

I NEVER DREAMED AS we neared my first-born child's high school graduation that we would be quarantined during a global pandemic amidst a backdrop of a personal catastrophe. Since everyone was out of school and work, we used this time to our advantage. Most of our days were spent knee-deep packing boxes and sorting through a lifetime of memories to move. At this point, I had decided to let the house go into foreclosure, and we had found a rental house to move into.

The kids were still wrapping their heads around separated parents, impeding legal issues for their dad, and moving out of their home. My daughter was also accepting that after busting her butt for the last four years and getting accepted to her dream college, she couldn't go due to our situation.

Being a high school senior during the 2020 pandemic held much pain and loss for many, but if my daughter had wanted to just give the world the middle finger, I can't say that I wouldn't have helped her. Seriously, all this loss, and now she gets to miss her final soccer season and all the other amazing moments that a high schooler looks forward to. As I held my first-born daughter almost eighteen years ago, of course I had hopes and dreams for her. Looking at her, though, I saw a blank canvas for God to paint on, and I knew He could paint something far more incredible than I could ever try to create for her. As time marched forward and she grew, I tried hard not to imagine what she would be like at eighteen. I wanted to watch her life unfold like turning the pages of a book, or watching the plot of a film revealed. However, this story had taken more than a few deep plot twists back-to-back.

My heart was devastated for her. She had been so strong through all of this, Uber driving her brother and sister while I worked at night, and she also set the tone for them. I didn't want to overburden her, but I'd been left with no choice but to let her grow up fast. In my heart, I knew that one day these lessons would serve her well, just as they had me, but I also didn't want the responsibility to break her before she had the chance to reap the rewards of early adversity.

Like most parents who had a senior in 2020, not seeing your kid walk across that stage was a hard blow. I mean, seriously, I endured twenty-four hours of labor, dropped off and picked the kid up over three thousand times, and packed over one thousand lunches. The least a parent is owed is to watch their kid walk across that stage to "Pomp and Circumstance." And after this year of hell, I wanted that more than ever.

A few weeks prior to the end of school, I had written this blog for her and her classmates:

> Your class of 2020 is currently experiencing the impacts of COVID-19. The picture you had imagined of your final senior semester is not to be. There will be no senior soccer

match, senior prom, senior skip day, and graduation will likely occur in a vastly different way. Not what anyone expected or planned.

This is not the first disappointment for you or your fellow classmates. Many of you have withstood trials that most of your peers will never know. As your mom, my instinct was to shield you from these events, but as a therapist I knew that your life would be enhanced by allowing you to navigate these difficult times. While no one wishes for trials, I am thankful that you have had some disappointments to help shape this view before you fly the nest.

As you and your classmates grieve through this disappointment, know that life will continue to bring you challenges. It is not how many challenges but how you choose to look at those challenges that will define each of you. While I know that I can never prepare you for all that life will hand you (aka a pandemic in your senior year), here are some things you and your classmates can bank on:

You will experience loss. Death and loss are a part of life, one that unfortunately our society likes to shield people from. When loss comes, allow yourself to grieve, whether it is a person, relationship, or goal. You do not always have to be the strong one. The intense pain of grief reflects the deep love that you shared. Know that you are never alone. The people you grieve for will surround you in a great cloud of witness that you will draw strength from in times of distress. They will become your roots and help you grow your wings. The dreams that you lose will often lead you to new doors that you never knew existed.

People will fail you and let you down. We are all broken people and will fail each other. This can occur within any type of relationship that you experience. Acknowledge the hurt to yourself and the person who hurt you. In time, seek forgiveness, and if appropriate, reconciliation. Do not let these disappointments allow you to become bitter and resentful or stop you from building new relationships and dreaming new dreams. That pain belongs to the past.

You will fail yourself and make choices you wish that you had not. This one will definitely be hard to believe at 18, but trust me, it will happen. Show yourself grace and get back on track. We are all human, fallible, so do not let these moments define you. Know that you are loved unconditionally, not for what you do but just for who you are. Use these moments to refine yourself and not allow these choices to become habits that lead to grave consequences.

You will feel bored, utterly lost, and confused in some stages of your life. Not every day will be exciting. You will often feel like you are on a hamster wheel or just on repeat. Not every day can be a mountaintop experience. Keep pressing on, try new things, and seek guidance from those who have traveled a similar path before you. Don't be afraid to try new things or think outside the box.

Give of yourself but do not be too proud to ask for help. We are meant to live in community with love and support from others. Your life will be made richer by giving of yourself, but we are not meant to do everything on our own. Seek help when needed. Allow yourself to experience the compassion and generosity of others. It will teach you humility and lighten the load.

Your faith will sustain you. No matter what people tell you, God does not bring the adversity into your life. He is your comforter, shepherd, and sustainer of your way.

Remember, He only promises two things: His unconditional love and the gift of eternal life. The end. Seek to do His will, and He will always show up for you. Often not in the way you wish or in your timing, but He will not leave you. We change, our circumstances change, but God remains the same.

There will also be plenty of good and lots of joy along the way. Soak it up and enjoy those seasons! No matter what happens, never stop dreaming. No matter how many times the waves knock you down, get back up and start again. The place that you arrive may not be the destination you had in mind, but if you learn to have a flexible mindset, it will be exactly where you are supposed to be in that moment.

The course is set ... now go ... run your race ... and always know that wherever you go, I will always be with you in spirit cheering you on.

"May joy and peace surround you, contentment latch your door, and happiness be with you now and bless you evermore!"

—An Irish Blessing for my tenacious redhead

As graduation time neared, it was a proverbial light switch. Graduation is on ... two days later, nope. As the class president, Landry had crafted her speech with little hopes of delivering it. Then we got the awesome news—outside, and with only two guests, but we were getting a graduation. Thank God, we finally caught a break!

It was a blazing hot June day with a threat of rain, but I didn't care. My husband and I walked to our seats, exchanging pleasantries with others along the way. Even though only a few people were aware of our situation, I felt so fragile, like everyone knew. Of course, a mom is going to cry at graduation, but this was just heavy grief. I looked around at her classmates whom I knew well and thought how broken all this was, and I was so hurt for my daughter.

Landry wouldn't let me see or read her speech prior to that day. I will never be able to tell her the depths of pride I had as she walked so confidently to that podium. I marveled at her composure, after everything she'd gone through. I thought no one would ever understand what she had struggled with on top of this pandemic.

As she begins, I am lost in a sea of memories: baby snuggles, a strong-willed two-year-old who told me that she was not going to use that potty, and I was a big bossy boiler (thank you, Thomas the Train), a precious elementary school child who stole the show as the twinkling star in a Christmas play, and now in a blink of an eye, this full-of-life red-head is a beautiful grown woman.

> "I believe the class of 2020 is the most resilient class WSE has ever had. To be resilient means to recover quickly from difficulty, and that's what we have done during this pandemic and the other trials I have mentioned. Resilience is perhaps the most needed trait in life. It is the strength to keep going, to keep fighting on, no matter the circumstances. On my graduation cap, or "mortarboard," as we learned in Mrs. Krochta's class, is a golden koi fish. Japanese legend tells the tale of a school of koi fish swimming upstream in the Yellow River in China. Once they got to a waterfall, most of the koi swam back, but after a hundred years, one was able to reach the peak of the waterfall. This koi was recognized by the Japanese gods for its perseverance, so they turned it into a golden dragon, the symbol of great strength and power. This is a symbol I

love and it is the perfect metaphor for what we've had to go through in our time here."

I smile. Hey, maybe she did learn something from all those counseling conversations. She continues.

"It has been an honor to serve as your president through this time. I wish my Presidential Committee and I could have done more to help, but during the Coronavirus crisis, we were limited to what we could accomplish. I am deeply sorry that there was no senior picnic, no senior skip day, no prom (yet), and no spring sports. These are things that you all deserved, and I hated to see them slip through my fingers too. But remember this: life will always be unexpected. You should never trust in what you want too strongly without remembering that sometimes we have to settle for what life gives us. It sounds like harsh advice, but this is the reality we live in. It's important to plan for the future but dangerous to attach ourselves to one future. What your life looks like today may not be what it looks like tomorrow. I certainly found that this year, with big changes in my personal life and now with the Coronavirus outbreak. You have to be willing to let go of what you want and recognize the new path that is best for you. Resilience and perseverance are not only about swimming against the current but sometimes going with it as well. Wherever the river goes, I put my faith in my God, and that is what helps me, because I know below the surface He has a plan for me, and it is going to be in my best interest, and He is looking out for all of you, my friends—even if you are unsure if He exists. I know this because He placed me in such a wonderful school with all the right people."

I can no longer see through my tears. I am simultaneously pierced that her worldview had to shift that fast, but also, I am completely blown away. At eighteen, she had learned something that would take most people a lifetime to embrace, if they ever do. As she finishes, I look up and thank God for every protective factor that has ever been woven into the lives of my children. Every teacher, coach, pastor, family member. Every single thread. They will likely never know that each of them sowed seeds that allowed her to endure the storm and come through with a few tattered sails but safely to the harbor.

As parents we won't always get the gift of reassurance that after we are gone our children can weather storms. We wonder if we ruined our kids over one decision or momentary anger. We beat ourselves up about so many things that won't even matter in the long run. What a gift that day to know that whether I'm here or not, or what comes her way, she will make it. That's the beauty of human resilience, and there is no greater gift for me.

Resilience Skill: Protective Factors

List your protective factors in your life. Write a letter of gratitude to them. If they are living, ensure they receive a copy, either handwritten or digital.

The Last Goodbye

"If you're brave enough to say goodbye, life will reward you with a new hello."

—Paulo Coehlo

ASK ANYONE WHO HAS been through loss, especially the loss of a spouse, and they will tell you that often the second year is the hardest. In retrospect, it makes sense, because in the beginning there is so much to handle related to their death legally, financially, and materially. These menial tasks, along with the shock, shield us from the crushing grip of the soon-to-hit reality. The person we loved is never coming home.

It was easy to miss the impending pain because hitting the one-year mark felt like such a victory. I literally felt like an Olympic runner breaking the finish line. Sigh … I made it, now where is my gold medal? So many of the things I had feared were either over or had thankfully never occurred. I was still singing in praise for being able to sell our house versus losing it to foreclosure. The profits had eased my financial stress significantly.

Over the first year, my days were consumed with working endless hours and looking out for my kids. Not to mention the time and energy that we all put into cleaning out and packing up our house. It's amazing what you can collect over the years. Not to mention that with the early passing of my parents, I had an attic full of family photos and heirlooms that had never been sorted. When we weren't at work or school, we were in constant motion packing or unpacking things. No matter my experiences with so many grieving clients, I never expected that darker times could exist beyond what I had already experienced in this first year of hell. Sorting through every single photo, piece of furniture, clothing, and fragment of your life, all while deciding what to keep and what goes, is like grief upon grief. If there was a deeper pain than what I felt that sweltering July day watching all of our family memories walk out the door of our home for pennies on the dollar at a yard sale, trust me, I didn't want to feel it.

As we started year two post disaster, we were settling into what the kids called our swamp house. It received this enduring name because literally in the first few weeks after moving there, a torrential rainfall caused the waters to rise and surround the house. Not to mention the frequent household visitors of frogs, snakes, and other miscellaneous swamp creatures. Even as the world was still dealing with COVID, the four of us were finding our new normal. We were all doing a hybrid of online and in person work and school. We began to cook and share meals and watch our favorite shows together. While different, it was beginning to feel like home. After a year of straight up survival mode, it felt like we were actually living again. Hope was rising that maybe, just maybe, we would be OK.

Despite this sense of hope, my grief and depression began to intensify day by day. Medically there is a condition known as broken heart syndrome. It's a temporary heart condition that is often brought on by stressful situations and extreme emotions. People with broken heart syndrome may have sudden chest pain or feel as if they're having a heart attack. Although in some cases it can be fatal, for most people it resolves quickly with proper treatment. This isn't the case with the emotional side of the broken heart. The waves of grief come over and over, like labor pains that never produce a result. When the waves subside, you're relieved to feel no pain, but the presence of joy is also nowhere to be found.

No matter the reason, divorce is painful. At times, it felt worse than if he had died. If he were dead, I would have no choice but to build a life without him, but he wasn't dead. It was a constant battle between my head and heart. I knew that I couldn't rebuild a life with him, but I didn't know how to have a life that didn't consist of him. When two lives have been intertwined for half your life, it's literally like trying to separate conjoined twins.

One night I just didn't know how I was going to move forward. What would have been our twenty-third anniversary was approaching, and I broke my pledge to the Magnolia Tribe and texted him. I wanted to know how he did it. Was it just that easy? He had been seeing a new person for several months now. So is that the answer, get a new person and move on? He wanted to meet and talk. Although I knew better, because this is how an emotional abuser wears you down, I agreed to meet him at the park the week of our anniversary.

Initially, I was on my "A" game. I was completely prepared, and he wouldn't break me down. It was a lot of back and forth with the same issues—him trying to defend his actions, and me still trying to get him to see my perspective. Our situation was so complex and hard. For most couples who divorce, there's often either a history of conflict or extreme disconnect, but ours had just been a sudden complete break that I never saw coming. It's like the whole world had moved on and we were just frozen in this awfulness. To me it felt like we had worked so hard to stay connected and keep our marriage a priority, yet here we were about to be divorced—the last of any of our friends that I thought would ever be divorced. My brain just couldn't reconcile the two experiences. No matter what you've been through, it's difficult to let go of these bonds. As we left, we hugged, and as I walked back to my car, I thought, *Wow, how sad to think that after sharing a lifetime of memories, this is how it all ends, with one last tearful goodbye.*

Irreconcilable Differences

"And he said to them, 'I am deeply grieved, even to death; remain here, and keep awake'"

(Mark 14:34)

AS OCTOBER FADED INTO November, we were nearing the date that I could finalize our divorce. Every day I was sinking deeper into the well of depression. I began to question my decision to divorce and to wrestle again with myself and faith about if I was making the right choice, running the same thoughts through my head over and over. People make mistakes. Is my bar for him too high? On and on the constant beating myself up, coupled with the debilitating grief. And here comes the holidays again. Yes, this is a winning combination.

After weeks of back-and-forth conversations and meetings, I had decided I needed to know that I had exhausted all options for this marriage. Even though the mental health professional was internally shaking her head and flashing a neon stop sign, and the Magnolia Tribe literally had stitches in all their tongues from remaining silent, my human heart needed to do anything to stop this gushing pain. It had been over a year, and I saw no relief in sight. I had to know that I had given this every chance.

Over the last few months, he had connected with a couple of men with similar situations who had served prison time with wives that stood by them. While on one hand I couldn't believe I was even entertaining staying in this marriage, I was desperate to find a solution to my pain.

Finally, I agreed to meet with one of the men and his wife on a Friday to discuss their experiences while their spouse was incarcerated. With COVID still raging, I was mostly working from home. It was a typical day, which consisted of working my day job, managing three kids, and then jumping on several telehealth sessions until about nine at night. My husband, who was working one job with no children living in his house, was texting me all day, wanting me to talk with him that night. I remember standing in my kitchen in the swamp house, full panic attack in motion, looking around at this house that I never would be living in and working myself into exhaustion and thinking, "Girl, please, what are you thinking? I don't care how long you were married; this man has put you and your children in this situation, and you are about to wait for his sorry butt to get out of prison? Who are you? Wake up!"

Even though I knew there was no way for me to ever trust or be married to him, it was still difficult to bring the divorce to a final close. I married for life and believed in this concept. No matter how much you know it to be right and are ready to move on, signing that one last piece of paper is very emotional. This event that was supposed to make me feel free made me feel more depressed. Now that I knew for sure that I couldn't rebuild a life with him, I still felt no hope for my future. I could hear all the cheerleaders in my head: "You deserve so much better. God is going to open so many doors for you." It all sounded like cliches; easy for all of you to say … your life is still intact. My literal soul has been ripped out.

Post-traumatic stress disorder, or PTSD, is very unpredictable. Just as you can rarely predict a tornado, PTSD triggers and flare ups can be just as difficult to monitor. You can think that you're doing fine, and then the next thing you know you're in a full-blown episode. PTSD causes the amygdala, or fire alarm of the brain, to be very sensitive, so the slightest reminder of the trauma can set you off. For the most part, I was having a great day. If my current mood was described as a weather forecast, it would have been sunny with a slight chance of rain. I had just left the attorney's office and was headed inside the bank. I walked in, pressed the door, opened the first set of doors … *click* … then the second … *click*. As the second door closed behind me, the click echoed so loudly, I felt like there was no one else in there but me.

I immediately noticed a tingling sensation wash over me, but I was unaware of my rapid dissociation. I proceeded to walk up to the counter as if I was perfectly fine. The teller said, "May I help you?" I couldn't think. I saw her talking, but my brain wasn't processing. She repeated herself. "May I help you?" I wanted to say "No, I'm pretty sure you can't."

I tried to tell her what I needed, but I couldn't put it into words. I finally snapped and just yelled at her. "Just give me $40 in cash. I don't care how you do it. Just do it." I guess I can be thankful for all her customer service training, because she remained very calm with me. As she began to count out the money, everything went into slow motion. The very act of watching money being counted was triggering me. Suddenly, I was no longer present in the moment; the teller has been replaced, and I saw my soon to be ex-husband standing behind the counter counting the money. My mind had jumped back to August 8, 2019. I was frozen, paralyzed by the fear that I had finally snapped and there would be no going back. Suddenly, a day with a slight chance of rain has turned into a F5 tornadic event.

Resilience Skill:

Use weather forecasting to describe your mood to others for less vulnerability.

This section discusses suicide, and some people might find it disturbing. If you or someone you know is suicidal, please contact your physician, visit your local ER, or call the suicide prevention hotline in your location.

Worse than Death

"*I am hard pressed between the two: my desire is to depart and be with Christ, for that is far better; but to remain in the flesh is more necessary for you*"

(Philippians 1:23).

SUICIDE IS A SERIOUS public health issue. Each year, almost 45,000 Americans die by suicide. It's an equal opportunity killer, and there is no single cause for suicide. As stress exceeds the coping abilities of a person in distress or with mental health issues, suicide can be the devastating result. While we don't like to think about this, given the right circumstances, at some point in life we can all be at risk.

In the winter of 2002, I was full of excitement and anticipation as my husband and I awaited the birth of our first child. After spending four years struggling through my grief over the loss of my dad, I was finally opening myself up to the new joys in my life. I have no idea what I was doing when the phone call came that day, and it really doesn't matter because everything just stops. Time freezes. Nothing else matters in that moment except what you just heard. My mom had attempted suicide and was being transported to the hospital.

"It doesn't look good" were the words that echoed in my head as we began the three-hour ride to the hospital. I still remember that sinking feeling in the pit of my stomach, wondering if she would be dead before we could get there. What if we were too late? As the miles ticked by, the flood of emotions was overwhelming. One minute I was so angry at her. "How could she do this to me? How could she not want to meet her new grandchild?" Then the shock, coupled with the fear of losing her, produced a flood of tears. My heart was pierced with a deep pain as I realized the hopelessness she must have felt to take her own life. Thankfully, my mom did survive to hold all of her grandchildren, but even as a therapist and hearing her best explanations, I still couldn't grasp that level of desperation.

Suicidal ideation is difficult to explain to those who have never experienced it, even mental health professionals. My epiphany moment of understanding my mom's level of pain only came when my level of pain finally matched hers. My mom and I were both married to our husbands for over twenty years, and although our loss was for different reasons, the loss is unbearable. You get up each day and hope for less pain, but it's still there. In that moment of connecting our pain, I finally realized that suicide is not about dying—it is about the release from these feelings of pain. You just need the pain to stop.

It was New Year's Eve, and I was sitting in the swamp house alone. While everyone else was celebrating new beginnings and setting new goals, I was fighting to evade death. The kids were with their dad, and a stone-cold quiet house was not my friend. I just kept thinking *I can't do it one more day. I cannot ride these waves. I am physically, mentally, and spiritually exhausted. I can't meditate, walk, call a friend, do one more hour of therapy.* In that moment, nothing seemed that it would ever give me the resolution I would need. As one of my therapist friends so accurately describes it, your brain is literally trying to kill you.

All I could think about was what it would feel like to just slowly let life slip away and wake up in the arms of Jesus. The relief of no more struggle and the end of my pain. No more getting up and putting on my game face, keeping it all in line, and taking care of more than my fair share. I was too tired to fight, and there were no more tears left to fall. Suicide is surrounded by so much stigma and judgment, particularly in communities of faith. I can assure you that any believer who struggles with suicidal ideation is not having a crisis of faith. Conversely, they likely have so much faith that they believe that to be absent from the body and present in Christ is their only answer. The only person I knew who could understand my current level of pain was Jesus. I knew He could empathize with my hurt, as He felt this kind of tormenting emotional pain the night before his crucifixion. As Jesus anticipated the pain He would have to endure in body, mind, and spirit on the cross, He went through an intense spiritual battle. This crushing emotional weight caused him to experience a medical condition known as hematohidrosis, which is a real medical condition in which the pain literally causes a person to sweat blood. When the physical body can't handle the pain, something has to allow for the release.

I'm a fortunate survivor of suicidal ideation. I'm grateful for the divine intervention that saved me that night to allow me to be here for my children and the work that God has called me to do. Luke 22:43 holds a beautiful passage where an angel meets Jesus to comfort and encourage Him for the challenge ahead as He prays in the garden that night. I believe that God, having experienced the same deep human pain, summoned several guardian angels to protect me that night. While their faces weren't clear, their familiar embraces were unmistakable. With a reassuring presence, my mom, dad, and many more arrived to hold me, and I collapsed into the safety of their spiritual arms to live another day. Even today this pain, though less intense, from time to time still wells up. I tap into that sense of angelic envelopment again and know that no matter how intense, eventually the pain will subside, and a new day will arrive.

Justice

> "He has told you, O mortal, what is good;
> and what does the Lord require of you
> but to do justice, and to love kindness,
> and to walk humbly with your God?"
>
> (Micah 6:8)

NEW BERN IS A small riverfront town located in Eastern North Carolina where the Trent and Neuse Rivers empty into the Pamlico sound. A stroll through the streets reveals colonial homes draped in festive bunting, which pays homage to the Revolutionary War era history. This city served as our first state capital and knows a thing or two about resilience. In addition to the Revolutionary War history, they rebuilt after the great fire of 1922 and most recently in 2018, after Hurricane Florence ravaged the community. Over the last few years, this place has drawn me with a magnetic pull that I can't explain. Give me mossy oaks, colonial architecture, and a view of water and I'm a happy girl. This unique town has graciously offered me refuge, and many pages of this book were written all around this alluring town.

This morning, the chill of winter is in the air as I walk to my destination. I turn the corner and step onto the curb on Middle

Street. I marvel at the beautiful building that has been so skillfully designed to fit into the colonial architecture of New Bern. I button my coat, look at my watch, and sit down on the bench outside the federal courthouse. I have always had a healthy fear of the law, and being on the wrong side of it was something that gave me great fear. Still does. This is the courthouse where my former husband will face the judge and get his final sentence.

Since August 2019, I have watched this scene play out in my head with various endings and different emotions. Sometimes as I would think about it, I would believe that I wouldn't be able to tolerate the moment when it would come. Other times I felt complete indifference about his fate. I pull the folded pages from my bag and begin to silently read.

> "It is just a white-collar crime" is one of the most damaging statements ever created. Even the semantics used are different. Instead of stealing, we get fancier terms, like embezzling. Crime is crime. I think somehow when people say white collar crime it implies there are no victims. Where there is crime, there is always at least one victim. In the case of the crimes my ex-husband committed, embezzlement and fraud, there were many victims. My heart is burdened for all those that he lied and stole from, but as I have learned throughout this bone-weary process, the spouses and children are often forgotten victims. My case was no different.
>
> On August 7, 2019, I went to bed a happily married wife of twenty-two years with three teens. While no marriage is perfect, my husband and I had worked hard to build a good relationship. If you asked anyone who knew us, we were the last on anyone's list to ever divorce. We spent time together, we enjoyed each other's company, and we were passionate about serving together in our church and community. Our oldest was embarking on her senior year of high school, and

with the other two close behind, we were looking forward to the next stage of life without all the responsibilities of kids. Most importantly, I trusted my husband implicitly.

My husband has a degree in economics, and he worked in the financial industry. My strengths are in education and mental health. By nature, from early on in our marriage he managed our money while I looked out for all things education and health. He always consulted me on decisions, and things didn't seem out of the way. In addition to our family finances, I entrusted him to manage the finances of my private practice from 2011–2017. Any time I had questions about how we were doing financially, he reassured me we were fine. Like his other victims, he even went to the lengths to make documents to show me what I now know to be false amounts to ease my worries.

When I originally learned of his crimes, I was devastated and broken to think that my husband had felt so much pressure that he stole for his family. Now I know that's what he wants everyone to think, but what he did is way more calculated and deceptive than swiping some money.

I have invested twenty-two years of my life emotionally and financially into a marriage and have nothing to show for it. In fact, I am worse off than before. I'm now in my late forties and have no retirement and no partner to help support me over the next few years to finish launching our children into the world. In addition, I have worked a second job to pay down debts that he told me were either already paid down or that he incurred to cover up his crimes. Unlike the financial institutions he took from, there are no laws to make him repay me in restitution for what his crimes have inflicted, and no insurance policies against fraudulent spouses to make me financially whole again.

It's true that people make mistakes, and everyone deserves a second chance. However, a person's true character shows when they must own up to their mistakes. Over the last few years, the loving husband and father I thought I knew has shown little to no remorse for his actions and how they have impacted those he victimized. He also doesn't see me or his children as victims of his crimes. Not only has he not been helpful, but he has worked against us, causing our struggles to be worse.

It sickens me to think of all the hours and projects we worked on for social justice in our community and world—likely projects he used in his defense to show his humanity. Most of our projects involved marginalized communities who are so often taken advantage of by those in power. All the time he was doing the very behaviors we were fighting to protect others from. It is so unconscionable, and I still can't wrap my mind around it. He led Bible studies on integrity and participated with his kids in Y guides and Indian Princess programs. I mean, if you can't trust that person, who can you trust? This type of criminal makes you never even ask the question, "Should I trust him?" Rather, you find yourself asking, "Why wouldn't I trust him?" In my opinion, this is the worst kind of criminal … the kind you trust.

As a mother, I knew that I would have to protect my children from many things in this life, but protecting them from their father was never one of them. In my situation, I am very fortunate that although this has been very difficult, I have education, a deep support, and privilege on my side. Many women and children in my situation will fall into poverty or never be able to rise out of poverty because of these types of crimes. This letter is not so much for me but to be a voice for the thousands of women and children that will be impacted long after I rebuild my life. I don't know what the answer is, but there must be some accountability and acknowledgment of the impact these white-collar crimes leave on women and children in the sentencing of these perpetrators.

This was the victim's statement I had intended to read that day in court, but I decided that for me, I needed to carry out justice in my own way. If I read this letter in the courtroom that day, the impact would be minimal, only reaching the ears of those in that space. No, I needed to find a way that not only brought me closure but made the greatest impact possible. I have always believed if you learn something, you should use it to help others to the greatest capacity you can. You are holding my justice in your hands.

Within the first few weeks of my life falling apart, I was visited by a spiritual mentor. She listened compassionately and then looked at me and said, "Melissa, you're not going to like or want to hear what I have to say to you right now, but one day you will understand. I have one word for you: opportunity. This experience is going to open doors for you and allow you to do things that, were it not for this experience, you could never do."

Would I choose to have my old life and marriage back? One hundred percent. Would I choose to have my parents live longer? Absolutely. I have certainly learned that loss and change are inevitable in this life, and with that comes an ongoing process of learning to adapt and change. A constant dance of reinventing oneself from the ashes. I walk over and place the letter in the trash. It has served its purpose; time to let it go and move forward. Pulling my coat snugger against the breeze, I begin the short walk back to my house. I take in one more glance of the complete tranquility and stillness of the river, and then I observe a very distinct smell. Yep, I have smelled that scent before, and it's most definitely the smell of opportunity.

Acceptance

"You've always had the power my dear, you just had to learn it for yourself"

—Glinda the Good Witch, The Wizard of Oz

ACCEPTANCE IS A HEAVY word. While grief truly never ends, this is the final formal stage of the grief cycle. Accepting that our life has been forever altered doesn't mean that we like the ending; it just means that we've come to terms with embracing a move forward in a new direction. It has been over thirty years since I sat on these banks at Carter Falls. I've returned to my roots in Wilkes County to reflect on the last few years and open myself up to new beginnings. The water gently washes over the rocks as the leaves slowly float from the trees, landing in the water to begin a journey downstream. A fitting image for where I find myself today, letting go of somethings and searching for the courage to begin anew.

As I allow the rush of water to lull me, I can hear the faint echoes of days gone by. These falls hold powerful memories with my cousins as we would sneak off to explore and cool off here on hot summer days. Just kids, living in the moment and splashing the day away, not a care in the world. I chuckle at how different childhood was in the early 1980s. We set off from home with no communication device, and to reach this pristine spot, we crossed several roads. Not to mention we were swimming unsupervised with no flotation devices. We likely only survived because of all the guardian angels around us.

I marvel at the absolute beauty of these falls and how small I feel in the universe compared to this force of nature. There is no one here but me, and I take in all the sounds and no sight of modern life. This water and these rocks were here long before me, and they will be here long after I'm gone. I feel my mortality the most in these spaces, probably because the absence of those gone before me is so strong. Yet another reminder that time is precious and fleeting, and, like most, I want my life to mean something after I'm long gone. I'd like to imagine that I could arrive at the end of my life and say, "I have no regrets." However, I'm pretty sure that not many humans get to that place. That should not even be the aim; rather, living a life of purpose should be the quest.

I wonder ... as that innocent child splashing in the water, did God see it all? Did He see my life before me with all the joys and pain? Or perhaps this all has been one great unfolding show to observe. The thought of predestination and that every moment is known is a bit scary to me, but alas the mystery of faith. I am reminded of the infamous philosophy debate about if you could know how and when you would die, would you want to know. I always said, "No way." I can also assure you that in all of life's unexpected events that have been joyous or devastating, I would not have wanted to know they were coming. I wouldn't have wanted the joy lessened or surprises ruined, and I would not have wanted to dread the horrible thing coming around the bend. I may never get all that figured out, but I believe that God is an ever-present force in my life, and that force allows me free will to choose many paths.

As I consider my purpose, my mind is spinning thinking about the dreams I had as a child and just how many unexpected things have occurred on my journey thus far. As this writing adventure has revealed, some of these things are incredible experiences, things that I never dreamed I would touch. Yet some of them are so heartbreaking that I wish I had no memory of the pain. In this moment, I acknowledge and give gratitude for all these experiences of my life because they made me who I am today. I am so thankful for all the times I said yes when it was scary. I can't imagine my life without being a dancer, without falling in love, without becoming a therapist or a mom, without Kenya and all the experiences with ZOE Empowers, without meeting Stella, without writing a book, without my public health school experience, without Guatemala, without Days for Girls, without Unearth Hope, and not to mention the beautiful people I have met along the way who are now a part of my story forever.

I sit here somewhere between the whispers of childhood dreams and the next chapter of my life. Today, I acknowledge the new desires that are beginning to bubble up in my heart like a hot spring. When I share my story with others, a very common remark is, "Oh Lord! Girl, I bet you will never trust another man." That trust pales in comparison to the trust I lost in myself. The greater question is will I ever trust myself enough and recover the sense of confidence that I had before? This experience cut me down to my knees by making me question my decision-making abilities, and it rocked my sense of safety to the core. Things that were once my greatest strengths became my areas of vulnerability. Here go the racing thoughts. Can I open myself up to new experiences that call to me? Can I find the brave me that is still somewhere inside, or will I continue to be paralyzed by fear? Can I risk it? Will I get hurt? What will I have to release to get what I want? Can I do it? What if I fail?

Past experiences tell me that even though I have stepped out of this proverbial boat before, it will require a daily process of calming those fears. As I wrestle with these thoughts of impending doom, I begin to sense a feeling wash over me, but I can't quite label it. This sensation arises out of thinking about what I might miss if I don't at least try to brave it out yet one more time. I don't want to miss the blessings for fear. I recall a favorite quote by Ambrose Redmoon: "Courage is not the absence of fear, but rather the judgement that something is more important than fear."

I am brought back to the present by a loud rustle of wind through the trees. The breeze envelops me like a familiar hug, and I feel safe and assured here, even after all these struggles. I see how God has used every piece of my life and now how fulfilling it is to acknowledge that all of my story has value. To see how God put desires in my heart that seemed crazy to me and others, yet they have come to serve a greater purpose. I open my Bible to read Psalm 37:1-5. This has been a deep source of encouragement for me, especially over the last few years

> "Do not fret because of the wicked; do not be envious of wrongdoers, for they will soon fade like the grass, and wither like the green herb. Trust in the Lord, and do good; so you will live in the land, and enjoy security. Take delight in the Lord, and he will give you the desires of your heart. Commit your way to the Lord; trust in him, and he will act" (Psalm 37:1-5).

> "Lord,
> I give you thanks for bringing us through this fire. Only you see the rest of the plan, and while I know it will contain more trials, I also know that you desire good things for me and my children. Give us hope to embrace possibilities and strength to face the challenges that lie ahead. Like the water that flows to carry the leaf on its journey, help me bend to your will and continue to grow and serve wherever you send me."

As the sun is near setting, I close my Bible, place it in my pack, and begin the short hike back to my car. The path from the falls to the car is a much easier path than thirty years ago, thanks to installed steps and other improvements. Good thing, since I'm no longer walking around in the body of an eight-year-old. This frame has a few miles on it. As I near my car, I notice the same wave wash over me from before. I finally can label that feeling. I let out a deep breath and acknowledge the feeling of peace. Welcome back, my old friend. I look up and see a sky full of bright and twinkling stars. Here, with little artificial light, they twinkle bright like Christmas lights. I stop and truly focus on each of those stars. I imagine each twinkle to be someone I miss waving down at me from heaven—a reminder that peace is always available to me, no matter what storm is swelling around me.

What a gift to know that I can stop striving for perfection and no longer have to search for peace. After so much grief and searching for this holy grail, I have finally found it yet again. This journey has reinforced to me that peace is not just present by a waterfall, while gazing at the stars, or in my connection with others; it is within me every day. I just had to learn how to step back, give myself permission to stop running, and tap into it. A twisty and fraught path to arrive at this place, but a journey worth every step taken.

Epilogue

"I am confident of this, that the one who began a good work among you will bring it to completion by the day of Jesus Christ"

(Philippians 1:6)

I PUSH MY STUFFED bag into the overhead storage and collapse into my seat. I buckle my seat belt and finally let out a sigh of relief. As the plane begins to climb higher and my butterflies begin to settle, I give thanks to God for where I am today. Though my life looks nothing like the picture I had painted, He is faithful to His promises of restoring brokenness. For once in my life, I have accepted that I can't anticipate every next step in front of me. What a sense of relief to release all the fears and truly just go along for the ride.

Exiting the plane, I feel the wetness of a tear slide down my face. A few years ago, I never thought I would feel anything but pain and emptiness, and I certainly never believed that I would feel alive with passion for life or love again. While my experiences have made me keenly aware that in this life there will be deep sorrow to bear, I know there is also joy to be found. As I step off the plane and my eyes connect with my target, I smile and give thanks that God is a much better story writer than I will ever be.

To God be the Glory

Resources for deeper reading on topics discussed in the book

- Beattie, M. (1990). *The language of letting go.* Center City, MN: Hazelden.

- Blackburn, E. H., & Epel, E. (2017). *The telomere effect: A revolutionary approach to living younger, healthier, longer* (First edition.). New York: Grand Central Publishing.

- Burke, H. N. (2018). *The deepest well: Healing the long-term effects of childhood adversity.*

- Daniels, S., & Piechowski, M. (2009). Living with intensity. Scottsdale, AZ: Great Potential Press.

- Levine, P. A., & Frederick, A. (1997). *Waking the tiger: Healing trauma : the innate capacity to transform overwhelming experiences.* Berkely: CA: North Atlantic.

- Kubler-Ross, E. & Kessler D. (2005). On grief and grieving. New York: Scribner.

- Nakazawa, D. J. (2015). *Childhood disrupted: How your biography becomes your biology, and how you can heal.* New York, NY: Simon Schuster

- Parnell, L. (2010). *Tapping in. A Step-by-Step Guide to Activating Your Healing Resources through Bilateral Stimulation.* New York, NY: Rodale.

- Sapolsky, R.M. (2004) *Why zebras don't get ulcers: The acclaimed guide to stress, stress related diseases, and coping.* New York: St. Martin's Press

- Siegel,D., (2007) *The mindful brain: Reflection and Attunement in the cultivation of well-being.* New York: Norton

- Sutherland, R. & Yokley, R (2008). Emergency! Behind the scene. Sudbury, MA: Jones and Bartlett.
- Williams, M., & Penman, D. (2011). *Mindfulness: An eight-week plan for finding peace in a frantic world.* Emmaus, PA: Rodale Books.
- Van der Kolk, B. A. (2015). The body keeps the score: brain, mind, and body in the healing of trauma. New York: Penguin.

CPSIA information can be obtained
at www.ICGtesting.com
Printed in the USA
BVHW050234220622
640206BV00001B/3